The Kingdom of Amarugia

The True Story of Missouri's Country Kings

<u>Other Titles by Jonathan A Jones</u>

Moonlit Mayhem: Quantrill's Raid of Olathe, Kansas

Border War Tour

An American's Guide to European Travel

Hippie War: Battle for the Harrisonville Square

All titles can be purchased at

www.JonathanJonesAuthor.com

The Kingdom of Amarugia

The True Story of Missouri's Country Kings

Jonathan A Jones

The Kingdom of Amarugia: The True Story of Missouri's Country Kings
2024 Edition
©2024 Jonathan Jones, All Rights Reserved
Printed and bound in the United States of American

For information contact Floating Spark Publishing
1660 N Hunter Dr
Olathe, KS 66061
www.JonathanJonesAuthor.com

admin@JonathanJonesAuthor.com

Available in these formats:
ISBN: 979-8-9874297-3-0 (Paperback)
ISBN: 979-8-9874297-4-7 (Kindle)
ISBN: 979-8-9874297-5-4 (E-Book)

Library of Congress Control Number: 2024911706

Although the author and publisher have made every effort to ensure the accuracy and completeness of the information contained in this book, we assume no responsibility for errors, inaccuracies, and omissions, or any inconsistency herein. Any slights of people, places, or organizations are unintentional.

This book is dedicated to my family, Jill, Zac, Lexi and Nikai.

Love you guys.

Acknowledgements

Jill Jones
Lexi Jones
Jennifer Healy, Editor
Polly Blair, Editor
Cass County Historical Society
Cass County Library

Special Thanks

There are too many people that I interviewed to thank them here. Their names, if they wanted them to appear, can be found in the references section at the back of the book. I would like to offer a special thanks to a few people who went above and beyond to help me gather information.

Danny Sanders
Steve Hamilton

Advanced Readers
Matt Brown
Patrick McWilliams

Contents

Sources

The first thing that readers should understand about Amarugia is that it is a place with no official boundaries, government, or citizens. Every person with any knowledge of the area likely has a different definition of the place and what happened there. That said, when looking for sources to tell the story of the Kingdom of Amarugia (Am-er-oo-gee), I was able to find a wide variety of sources that added to the history and lore of the area. Amarugia is described in the July 1990 edition of the *Missouri Conservationist* this way, "Legends and folklore grow as thick as the oaks in the rolling hills and are as mysterious as the boundaries that separate the hill people of Amarugia and their neighbors, the prairie people." (*Missouri Conservationist*, pg. 14)

Without a doubt, the primary source for any work about Amarugia is Donald Lewis Osborn's 1972 book, "*Tales of the Amarugia Highlands*". All research done on Amarugia in modern times, including mine, has to start with Osborn's book. *Tales of the Amarugia Highlands* is a short, 30-page, 81/2 X 11 book full of Osborn's interpretation of newspaper articles and personal interviews about the area. The book is difficult to locate and is not available through most of today's normal distribution methods. Osborn, who grew up in the region, says that the material for the book was "based on tales he had heard from his mother as a child as well as 'interviews, newspaper clippings, plat books, deeds and other documents and cemetery research.'" (*Daily Journal*, 1987) The book is full of interesting stories and tales, some of which can be loosely verified and others that cannot. This work will include many points that come from Osborn's work. I want to emphasize that the only reason that there is even enough information to attempt to tell the story of Amarugia is due in large part to Osborn's work.

While Osborn was the first to bring the data together in order to tell the story, most, if not all accounts of the kingdom are derived from three articles printed in Cass County newspapers. The first, written by John Wooldridge, was printed in the *Cass County Times* in February of 1887. This article was then reprinted and added to by an unknown author in by the same newspaper, now called the *Cass County Missourian*, in 1889. Sixty years later, another story, written by Donald Bradley, was published by the same newspaper in 1949. The 1949 article, like the 1889 article, includes most of the 1887 article, again reprinting most of the text. These three articles provide most of the history of the lineage of the kings of Amarugia. You are probably very confused at this point, and in an attempt to clarify, just remember that there were three articles printed over time by the paper that would eventually become the *Cass County Democrat-Missourian* that are used as primary sources. For text citations, I have attributed most items to the 1949 article as the three articles contain much of the same information.

Figure 1: Cover Image of Donald Osborn's book, Tales of the Amarugia Highlands.

Another significant source for this book is a book titled, *Amarugia*, written by Robert L. Gross, in 2009. Gross grew up in Amarugia and writes this fictional account of two young boys growing up in the area around 1911-1915. This book is classified as juvenile fiction but is a must-read for anyone trying to get a picture of what life was like in that era in Amarugia.

The story that Gross creates is one full of life lessons for youth along with a heavy dose of religion, which makes sense given Gross's occupation as a missionary for most of his life. Gross weaves in folklore and events that likely happened during the author's childhood in Amarugia. In some instances, it appears that historical timelines are fudged a bit to ensure that a story can be told from the vantage point of our two young heroes. These timeline discrepancies don't really impact the story and to be fair, will likely go unnoticed by the adolescent readers of Gross's book. One thing I will note is that Gross's book does provide what I feel is the best map of the Kingdom of Amarugia. I have been able to transfer Gross's hand-drawn map into modern-day mapping software. This map will be presented in a later chapter.

Figure 2: Robert L. Gross, author of the juvenile fiction book, Amarugia, published in 2009.

In addition to the aforementioned books, there are many newspaper articles that mention Amarugia, some dating as far back as 1884. Many of the early articles came from the *Cass County Democrat-Missourian*, or other Cass County newspapers. In the Cass County papers during the 1890 – 1910 timeframe, a reader would find Amarugia mentioned in the reporting of various incidents and more commonly the Amarugia social scene. Small town newspapers of this time would generally include a small section for each of the towns in the area the paper covered. These social sections would report on important topics such as who went to visit family in Harrisonville, or which families got together for Sunday lunch after services the previous week.

Mention of the Amarugia social scene and various other events by the newspapers of the time is interesting because it shows that the concept of the area known as Amarugia actually exists. This is in stark contrast to the 1883 and 1917 History of Cass County publications.

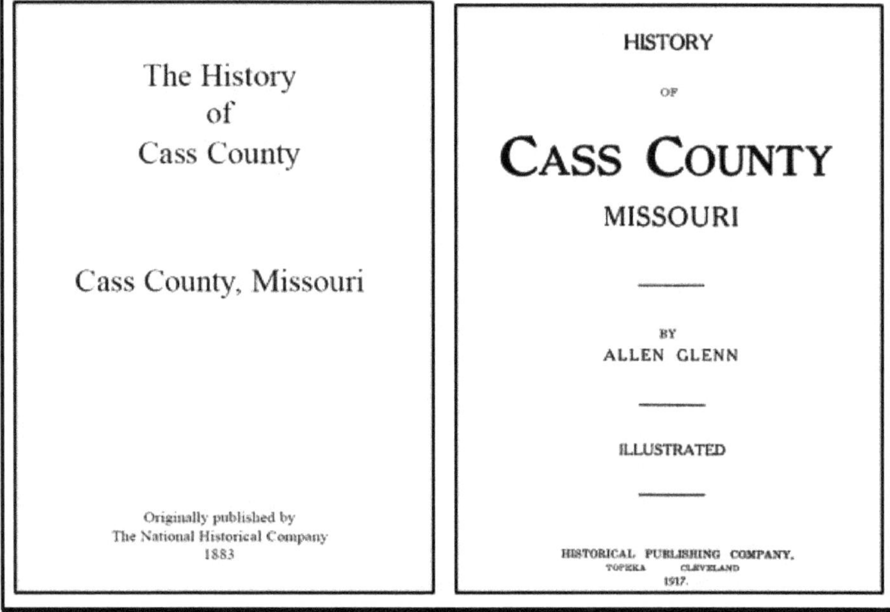

Figure 3: Cover images of the 1883 (left) and the 1917 (right) History of Cass County. Neither publication contains the word "Amarugia".

which contain absolutely no mention of Amarugia. The fact that Amarugia is regularly mentioned in the newspapers tells us that the county residents of the time used the moniker frequently to refer to the area. It seems a bit odd, that local historians and authorities apparently did not feel that this area warranted any sort of mention in the history of the county.

By 1923, the mention of Amarugia in local newspapers had stopped. This likely coincides with the people of the region ceasing to refer to themselves as Amarugians. From a historical standpoint, you might attribute this to the fact that citizens were becoming more mobile and were not as "confined" to the area where they lived. It could also be attributed to the fact that this is roughly when it appears that the concept of the "kingdom" had fallen out of favor.

Amarugia is rarely mentioned in any written publications between 1923 and 1970. In the 1970s the topic of Amarugia got a second life when the story emerged that in the mid-1800s and early 1900s the area was reportedly governed by a "King". When Osborn's book was published in 1972, it seemed to give the story of the Kingdom of Amarugia a whole new life, as many articles would be written in the next several years bringing renewed attention to the story.

It is the intention of this book to attempt to enhance, with modern research tools and sources, the work done by Osborn, Gross, and a host of newspaper writers over the past 100 plus years. The reader should realize that many of the incidents reported in this book originated via word of mouth and are pulled from stories told around the campfire or family hearth.   Most of the storytellers who were passing these tales along have long passed away and are no longer around to confirm certain details of these stories. Exact dates are scarce when discussing Amarugia and while every attempt has been made to ensure that dates line up with known historic events, there are some things that are simply "best guesses". Such is the history of "Amarugia".

I also want to note that I have taken some liberties regarding the format of in-text citations. The proper MLA format is to list the author's name, or if that is not available, the first word in the article title, then the page number where the information can be found. This allows the reader to easily track the citation back to the source in the bibliography. While writing this book I realized that many of the articles I was citing had no author and no title as they were simply small notices in newspapers.   This meant that many of the citations might say (Amarugia, 1) which does not distinguish this source from a different article with the same title. For this reason, I have replaced page number with full or partial dates to make clearer the exact source from which the note was derived. I'm sure my high school English teachers will be furious, but I think this is the best way to clarify the various sources.

History of Cass County

Cass County, Missouri is located just south of Kansas City, Missouri and is considered part of the Kansas City metropolitan area. The largest towns in the county include Harrisonville, the county seat, Belton, Pleasant Hill, and Raymore. The population history of the county is shown in the table below:

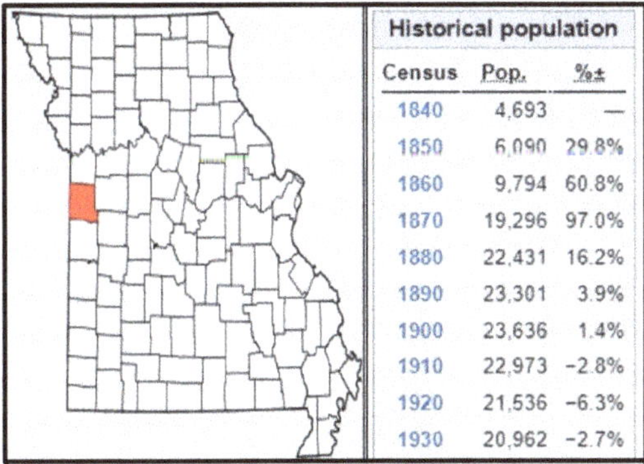

Historical population		
Census	Pop.	%±
1840	4,693	—
1850	6,090	29.8%
1860	9,794	60.8%
1870	19,296	97.0%
1880	22,431	16.2%
1890	23,301	3.9%
1900	23,636	1.4%
1910	22,973	-2.8%
1920	21,536	-6.3%
1930	20,962	-2.7%

Figure 5: Image on the left shows the location of Cass County on the western border of Missouri. The

Missouri was originally part of the Louisiana Purchase in 1803 and became the 21st state in the Union when it was admitted to the United States as a slave state under the Missouri Compromise in 1821. Cass County was officially formed in 1837 and at that time was called Van Buren County after President Martin Van Buren, who served as the President of the United States from 1837-1841. Until 1849, Van Buren County covered the land that now makes up Cass and Bates counties. In 1849, the county was split, and two new counties were formed with neither wanting to maintain the Van Buren name. Van Buren had become extremely unpopular in southern leaning western Missouri. His political views had shifted over time to a pro-abolitionist viewpoint

Figure 4: 8th President of the United States, Martin Van Buren. President from 1837-1841.

which conflicted with the viewpoint of most of the pro-slavery residents in the county at the time.

Due to the general dislike of Van Buren, and his pro-abolitionist views, the residents decided to rename the county in 1849. The decision was made to name the county after Michigan Senator Lewis Cass who was a two-time cabinet member and failed presidential candidate in 1848. Cass, a slaveholder, was a leader in the Doctrine of Popular Sovereignty, which was a belief that each state should be allowed to choose whether or not to allow slavery.

Prior to the Civil War, the county was predominantly pro southern and thus pro-slavery. After the Civil War, due to harsh reconstructionist policies implemented in Missouri, the county population shifted to a more balanced political split. Many of the pro-Confederate residents were forced to

Figure 6:   Lewis   Cass,
Michigan   Senator   and
namesake of Cass County,

leave the area when the reconstructionist government required all residents, many of whom had been forced out of their homes due to Order Number 11, to pay four years of back taxes if they wanted to keep their property.

What is an Amarugia?

The origin of the name Amarugia is far from clear and there are many theories regarding where the name may have originated. The *Cass County Democrat-Missourian* suggests with no backup, that the word means "an unsavory place" (History, 1849). Osborn suggests in his 1972 book that it may be a combination of the Greek words "ambrosia" and the name of a Greek town "Amarousian". He also presents another possibility that because the Indians were the first occupants of the land, the name may have been derived from a Native American word, meaning "distasteful or bitter". Osborn's research contends that if it was derived from an Indian word, it would likely have been from the Omaha-Osage-Ponca-Quapaw line of the Sioux family of tribes. This logic is valid since the Osage Indians were the primary residents of Amarugia before white settlers came to the area. (Osborn, 2)

In a "letter to the editor" sent from an Amarugia resident and printed in the *Cass County News* in 1900, the letter's author implores readers to, "Study ancient history and your Bible and you will find that a long time ago there was a very fertile valley in Egypt called Amarugia." (Letter to Editor, 1900) This makes it clear, that at least in the year 1900, some residents of Amarugia felt that the name was derived from this Egyptian valley. I have not been able to uncover any mention of Amarugia, or anything close to it in any biblical sources. Of course, there are different versions of the Bible and the fact that I could not find it doesn't mean it isn't in some version, but I did not find "Amarugia" in any modern version of the Bible.

One more possibility, just to muddy the waters a bit, is a reference in Incan mythology of South America, to a creature known as the "amaru". The amaru is a dragon-like animal of Incan lore, which sported the heads of both a puma and a bird. It is often depicted with wings and feet. Legend says that this beast was a "powerful creature with a fox's mouth, a fish's tail, a

Figure 7: Sketch of the mythical creature,

snake's body, scales, and sometimes wings." It was found frequently throughout Andean iconography and naming within the empire, and likely predates the rise of the Inca." (Amaru)

So where did the name come from? Take your pick. We will never know for sure. If I had to place bets, my wager would be that the most logical answer as to the origin might be that it is derived from an Indian word. That said, none of the options can truly be ruled out. There is simply not enough evidence, for any of the options, to conclude with any certainty where the name may have come from.

Where was/is Amarugia?

As mentioned in the opening chapter, Amarugia is not a place that can be easily defined by drawing lines on a map. Amarugia is like the Ozarks, anyone asked to define the exact geographic area will likely have a slightly different definition of where the boundaries begin and end. One writer defined Amarugia as,

> **. . . a section of Cass County, southwest of Harrisonville, bordered on the south by simplicity, on the north by naturalness, on the east by earnestness, and on the west by wisdom – peopled by the descendants of Earls and Dukes and Kings..." (We Have Been, 1916)**

This description does not exactly lend itself to plotting it on a map.

Officially, at least according to government records, Amarugia did not exist. Instead, it was a name used by residents to describe a general area. I would equate it to how someone might refer to places such as Skunk Holler, Dogpatch, or Frazier's Ridge. The name Amarugia does not appear on any official documents, or plat maps, of Cass County until 1987 when the Amarugia Highlands Conservation Area

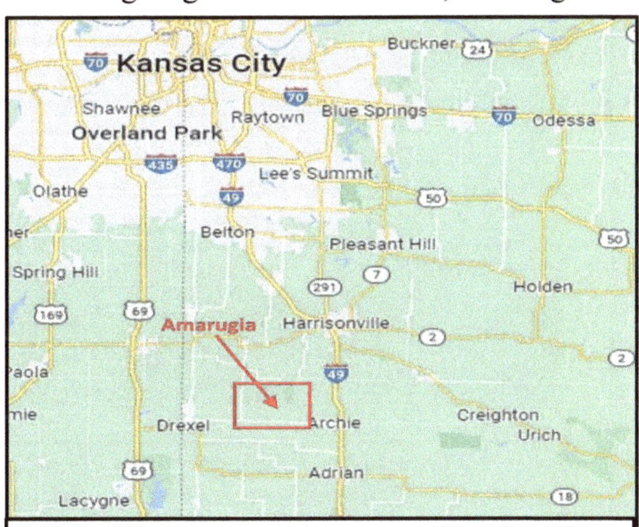

Figure 8: *Amarugia is part of modern-day Cass County which includes the towns of Belton, Pleasant Hill, Drexel, Harrisonville, and Archie These towns are shown on the map. (Courtesy Google Maps)*

was opened. The name "Amarugia" also never appears in any of the previously mentioned "Histories of Cass County". This is rather surprising since these "histories" of Cass County were written when the Kingdom of Amarugia was reportedly at its most prominent. Why then, is there no mention of it in any official publication?

Cass County is divided into seventeen townships. The townships are used as a mechanism to organize land records. Each township is then subdivided into smaller units which are arranged in a grid-like

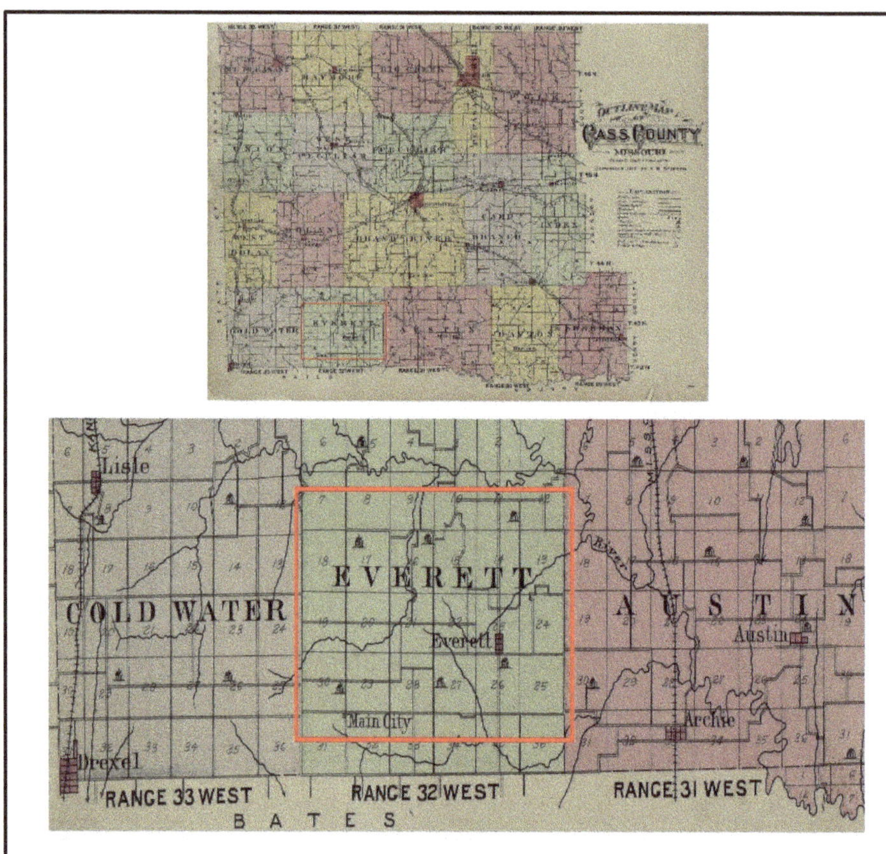

Figure 9: (Top) This is an image of the 1913 Plat map for Cass County. Bottom: The image on the bottom is a closer view of the same map showing the Township of Everett. Note the red square around "Everett Township" which shows a rough estimation of the boundaries of

pattern. You will see these numbers on the plat maps throughout this book. This method is used across Missouri and most other states as well. The kingdom of Amarugia was in Everett Township which is located on the southern border of Cass County. Everett Township is bordered to the west by Coldwater Township, Austin Township to the east, and Dolan and Grand River Townships to the north. See the 1913 township map above.

The exact boundaries of the kingdom are difficult to pin down. Over the years, various articles and publications have defined the boundaries of the area in various ways. A few of those descriptions are listed below in roughly chronological order:

- <u>King Owens I's official surveyor</u>: (approximately 1840) reported that the kingdom, "...... **extended northward as far as the South Fork of the Grand River. The southern boundary being limited by the commencement of the vast prairie lands of the Everett territory. Eastward as far as the confluence of the South and Middle Forks of the Grand River. Westward to plains of Brosley. (Reeves, pg. 17)**

This description, which originates from one of the earliest articles about the area makes the kingdom much larger than most of the other descriptions. "Westward to plains of Brosley" means that the kingdom goes all the way to Kansas/Missouri border and includes all of Coldwater township. Brosley was a town that ceased to exist in about 1870 and was situated in the very southwest corner of the county just northeast of where Drexel is today. The map below shows the boundaries as they were described in this description. This early definition of the kingdom is far larger than most later descriptions give it credit for. This may

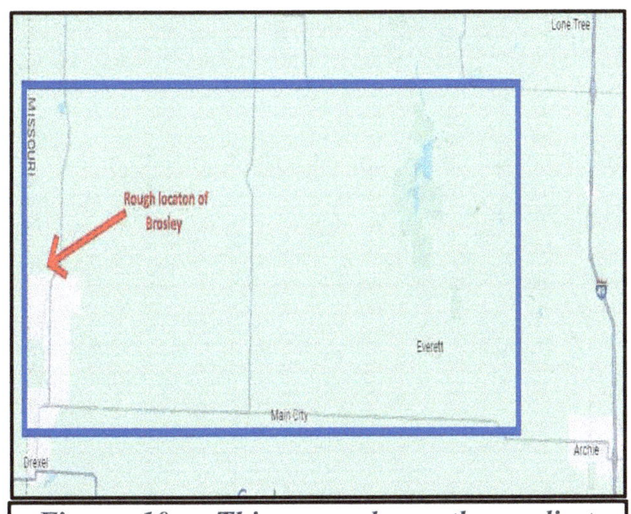

Figure 10:   This map shows the earliest description of the boundaries of the Kingdom. The town of Brosley no longer exists. (Courtesy Google Maps)

be attributed to the human tendency of men to claim more than what is theirs. In this case in the 1840s, there were very few people in the area, which meant there were very few people who might complain if the kingdom claimed more land than was actually under its domain.

- *Cass County Democrat*: (citing1849 article) "Amarugia is a neighborhood located between the south prong of Grand River and Owens Creek, in this county [Cass] (In Everett Township"). **This definition really doesn't make much sense since Owens Creek flows into the south prong of the Grand River. There is no area "between" the two.

- *The Missourian* (1952) "We of the Everett community felt that it [the eastern edge of Amarugia] was just west of Everett, in fact the Everett Cemetery was a nice dividing line." **This definition is likely from someone who felt that Amarugia was

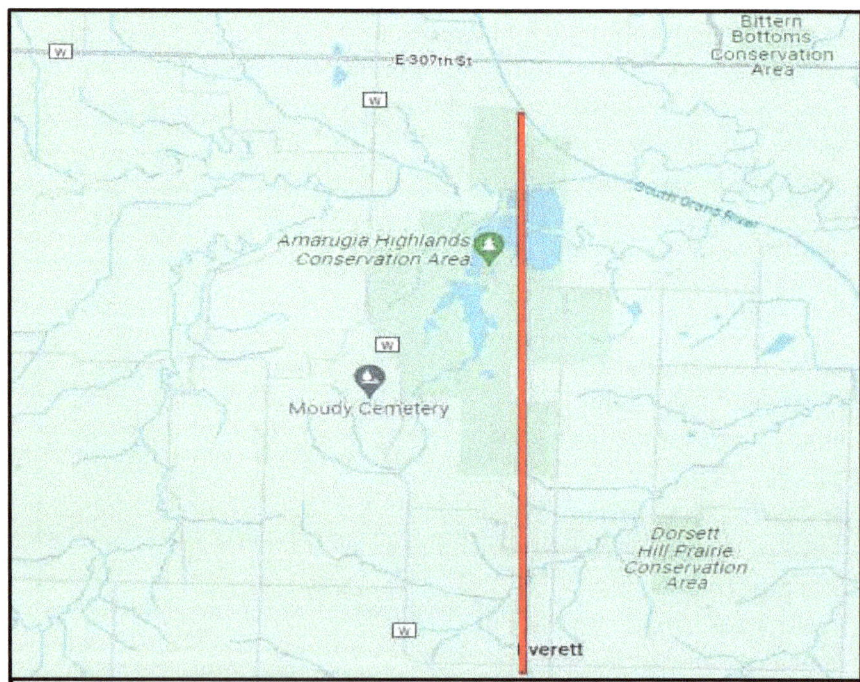

Figure 11: The line on map shows where this definition's eastern boundary would be located. This would match with one of the early ideas of the boundaries, but not with later definitions. (Courtesy Google Maps)

always "just over the hill". Note that they do not include the City of Everett. This definition will be disputed by King David's 1894 Proclamation which will be presented later.

- <u>Cass County Historical Tour.</u> (1972): Amarugia is centered around Christiansen's Mound, which was known at an earlier time as Scalplock Mountain. Christiansen's Hill is located just off today's South Amarugia Lane, just west of Moudy Cemetery. Osborn describes it this way: "Christiansen's Hill, so well-known for its round mound appearance—near which the Christiansen home stood until a few years ago." [in 1972] This was formerly the Davenport home where Jesse James and Cole Younger, the outlaws, are said to have stayed overnight with the Davenports and traded horses. You will see the Davenport name in a later chapter as a member of the family who played a key role in the naming of a king.

Figure 12: (On the left is a topographical view of Christiansen's Hill, also known as Christiansen's Mound, or Scalplock Mountain. The image on the right is an author photo, taken from South Amarugia Lane due east of the mound. It is private property and can only be accessed via a private drive. (Courtesy Google Maps)

- <u>Donald Osborn</u>. (1972) "The boundaries of Amarugia are controversial. Some say Amarugia is that land from which water drains into Owens Creek and its tributaries. This stream flows generally northeastward and empties into the South Fork of the Grand River". (Osborn, 2) I think this is a good definition of the Kingdom prior to King David's Expansion in 1894. This definition accurately describes the "Highlands", or the area where the "Hill People" lived.

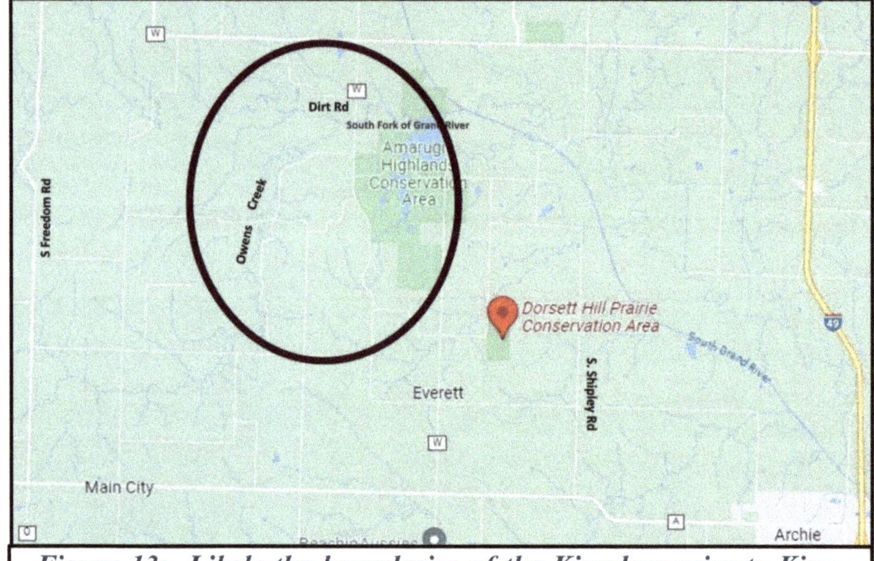

Figure 13: Likely the boundaries of the Kingdom prior to King Davids expansion in 1894. (Courtesy Google Maps)

The reality is that the boundaries of the kingdom have changed and morphed over the years based on who was attempting to describe the area. The boundaries were also changed by Royal decree, with King David's "Royal Proclamation" in 1894. This proclamation expanded the boundaries to the south and east so that the kingdom would include the town of Everett. This change came at a time when King David had just relocated from the Highlands to a house just southwest of the town of Everett. The king didn't want to lose the crown, so he simply moved the boundaries to include where he was living.

In my opinion, the best description is from the map published in Osborn's study, which shows the general area in which the kingdom was located. This map really doesn't attempt to define external boundaries but rather shows the general region that was considered the kingdom pre-1900. This general area logic is more consistent with how people thought of the kingdom at that time. This map also shows the location of the prairie, which was located southeast of the highlands. Originally, the prairie was not part of the kingdom, and residents from the prairie were enemies of the Amarugia residents. At this time, the area comprising the "kingdom of Amarugia" was referred to as the "Highlands". There is more information about the "Prairie People" later in the book. Most of the history and lore surrounding Amarugia is based around a map that looks like the one shown above. (Osborn, 3)

The following map is representative of the kingdom in the 1840-1870 timeframe. In this map you will see a road called "Dragoons Trace" that runs through the area. "Trace" is an old term synonymous with "road". According to Osborn, this was likely a military road used by the Federal soldiers during this period to assist them in managing the Indians that were still living in the area. This road would likely have been considered the eastern edge of Amarugia. (Osborn, 3) The City of Everett, founded in 1867, was not in existence at the time and is only shown on the map as a point of reference.

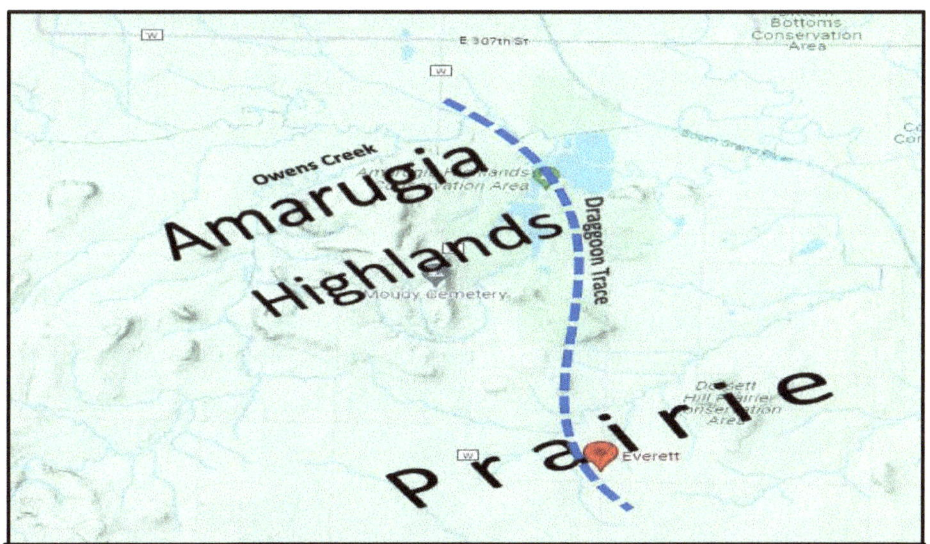

*Figure 14: This map is based on the map presented by Daniel Osborn in his book The Strange Tele of the Amarugia Highlands. (Courtesy Google Maps) *The map in Osborn's book does spell "draggoon with two "gs". That is not the proper spelling, but I have left the map as is.*

Finally, the next map below shows what is considered by many to be the boundaries of the kingdom of Amarugia today. Of course, the idea of the kingdom no longer exists, but many articles written about it, define it using these boundaries. This is probably far larger, particularly to the west and south, than the kingdom was in its heyday.

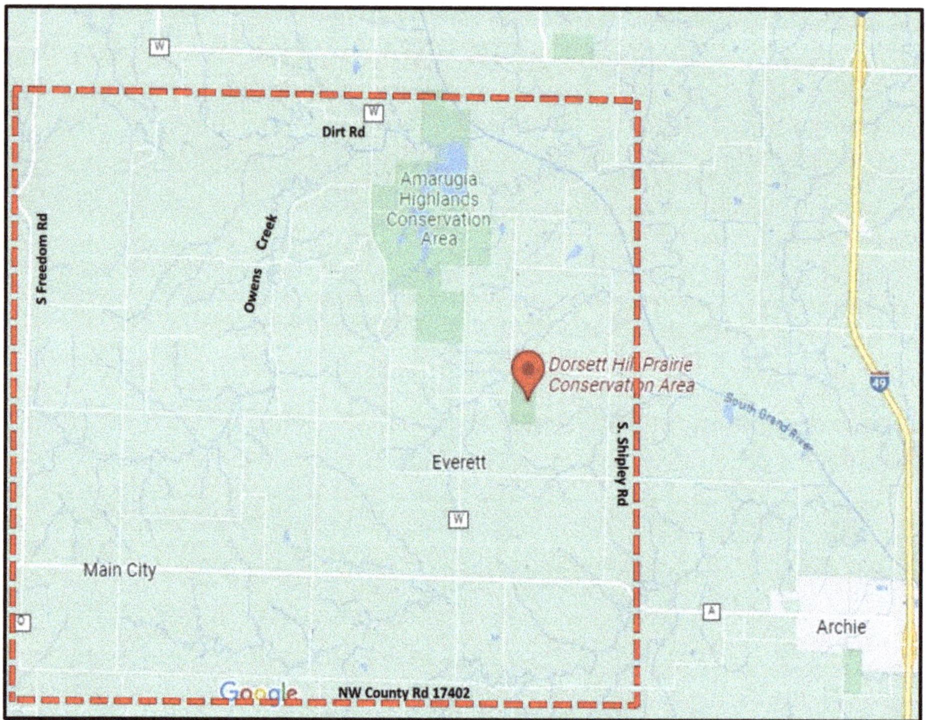

Figure 15: This image shows a Google Map of the area that comprised the kingdom, according to most contemporary writers. The red dotted line shows the imaginary boundaries of the kingdom with modern roads to give the reader a clear view of where the boundaries would have been located today. (Courtesy Google Maps)

History of the Royal Line per the 1887 Article

The exact history of the royal lineage of the kingdom of Amarugia is fuzzy at best. In this chapter I will do my best to detail the men who ruled the kingdom, detailing the historical persons who may have filled this role and showing the timeline of their reigns. There is no official record of the dates that each king ruled the kingdom, so the exact dates are a best guess using data derived from a wide variety of historical records. As previously mentioned, the characters in this story mainly come from oral histories that have been retold over time. The first written account of the kings' affairs is generally pulled from the previously mentioned *Cass County Times* article published in 1887, reprinted in 1889 and again in 1949.

Since then, several other articles on the topic have been published in a wide variety of publications. Some of the later articles changed some of the original facts without any documented sources for those changes. There is no way to prove if these changes were intentional and supported by research, or if they were simply mistakes that were picked up by other papers and eventually became the "truth". Think of the "telephone game" where a story is told again and again over the years and some of the key points of the story change from one telling to the next.

I have done my best to filter out what is blatantly wrong, but I will also let the reader know when there are questions about the information being presented. Through my own research, I have strived to identify the actual people that represent historical figures in the story. In some cases, I feel very good about the accuracy of who I have identified as a character in the story, and in others, there may be multiple people who could possibly have filled a certain role. Again, I will let the reader know when I am making "my best guess" regarding the facts.

Basey Owens, who is generally agreed upon to have been the first king of Amarugia, came to Missouri from Big Sandy, Kentucky, as an agent for the Hudson Bay Fur Company. Basey is generally recognized as one of the first full time residents of Amarugia after settling in the area in around 1830. In his role as a trader and trapper for the Hudson Bay Company, Owens set up a small trading post on the east side of what is now known as Owens Creek. (Lethcho, 50) It is logical to assume that it took several years for the trading post to grow into a community, the size of which led the residents to realize that they needed some form of government to manage their small settlement. The need to keep order prompted residents to form a committee with the task of deciding on a form of government for Amarugia. At this meeting, possibly in the 1840-1845 timeframe, the residents chose to implement an Absolute Monarchy. The committee further decided that the founder of the settlement, Basey Owens, would be crowned as King Owens I, the first ruler of Amarugia.

While things went well for the community and King Owens I for a while, at some point the fur bearing animals of the region became scarce and there was dissension between the people in the highlands and their neighbors living in the "prairie". The "Prairie People" were called

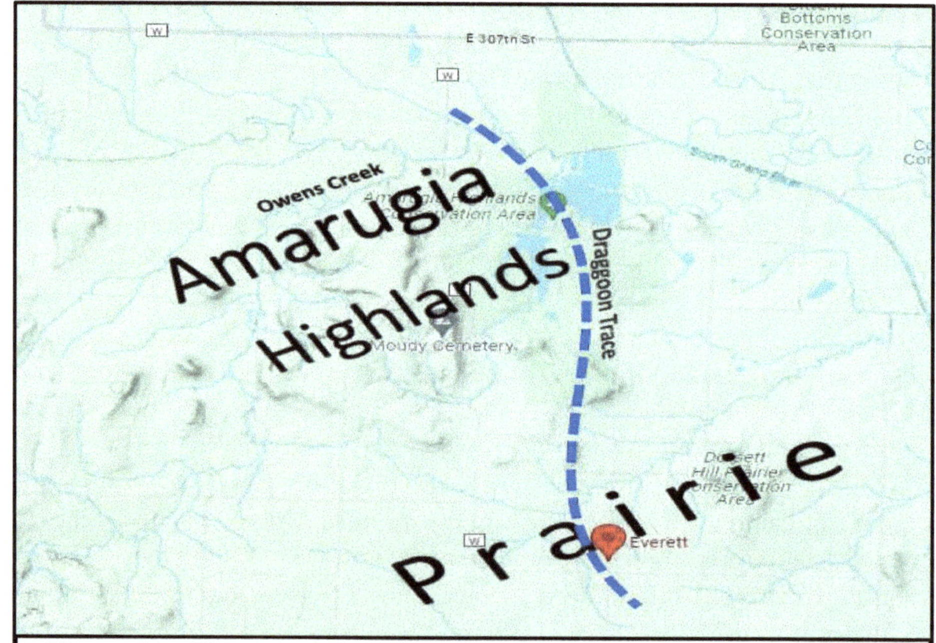

Figure 16: This map is based on the map presented by Daniel Osborn in his book The Strange Tale of the Amarugia Highlands, pages 10-11. (Courtesy Google Maps)

"Indianans", a term which is a bit of a mystery. It is certainly not referring to people residing in the state of Indiana, as that is just too far away and doesn't make sense. It also does not seem to refer to the term "Indians" denoting Native Americans from the region. The most logical explanation is that the people living on the "prairie" (see map below) were settlers who originally came from Indiana and were thus tagged as the Indianans. The territory of Indiana was established by the US Congress on May 7, 1800, and was granted official statehood on December 11, 1816. With those dates in mind, it is not too far-fetched to think that maybe the residents of the prairie had migrated from or were descended from people who lived in the Indiana Territory or State of Indiana.

After reigning for just a few years, King Owens I was kidnapped and held ransom by the "prairie people". According to legend, the kingdom opted not to ransom their king and King Owens I died after a few years in captivity. One account contends that he died of a "broken heart" brought about by his loyal subjects making the decision not to ransom him. The physical reason for his demise was likely disease as that was the most common cause of death in those times.

I have done extensive research trying to figure out the players in the Owens' family tree to pin down Basey's identity. My research comes from state and local archives, census records, genealogy websites, land and marriage records and newspaper articles. This sort of research is tricky and not fool proof. The genealogical sources, which are the best way to trace family lineage, are often populated by amateur genealogists. I don't want to criticize these folks, because I consider myself one of these amateur genealogists, having researched my own family heritage. That said, the problem with these types of sources is that mistakes are made and not corrected on the internet where subsequent researchers assume that the data is correct. These sites are kind of like Wikipedia, eventually someone will find and correct errors, but until someone corrects it, the error is out there and is treated as fact. In the next few chapters, I will detail the actual Cass County residents who I believe served as a King of Amarugia. I will present my logic as to the selection and explain why I was led to these conclusions. After each name, I will conclude with a "confidence index". This will show, in percentage form, how confident I am that I have found the correct historical person.

I have been unable to find anyone named Basey Owens in any historical records in Cass, then Van Buren County. It is possible that "Basey" is a nickname which would make him difficult to identify. It is also possible that since very few written records existed at this time

on the Missouri frontier, that records about Basey simply do not remain. I have found a man named Thomas Owens, who is listed as owning land in Section 9 in 1839, but the only thing that makes me think Thomas Owens might have been Basey, or King Owens I, is the timing of their presence in Everett Township.
<u>Confidence level that Thomas Owens was King Basey Owens I: 15%.</u>

The timing works, but there is just not enough information on either King Owens I or Thomas Owens to say with any confidence that this Thomas Owens was the man called Basey Owens.

If we estimate that Basey Owens' reign and captivity lasted around 10 years, that would mean that the next king took over around 1850-1855. After King Owens I's demise in captivity, the kingdom named King Owens II, a descendent of King Owens I, to be the new king. The term descendant could mean anything from father, uncle, grandfather, etc. The 1887 account tells us that King Owens II, with the assistance of an elected council, redirected the energies of the kingdom away from the fur trade and toward agricultural endeavors. For several years after his ascension to the crown, the region continued to clash with their neighbors to the southeast, the Indianians. The newspaper story tells us that the kingdom struggled for many years with. . .

. . . petty warfare was waged by the clans living along the boundary between Amarugia and the prairie. The Indianians encroached upon Amarugia soil, killing their game, stealing their wood, and 1,000 other depredations, to which the Amarugians hoped to retaliate by stealing their chickens and an occasionally a fat hog." (History 1887)

King Owens II reigned for many years although his reign was plagued by the same political issues with "other Kingdoms" as those that plagued his predecessor. It is said that King Owens II died of old age after a long reign.

I believe that it is possible that King Owens II could possibly be a man named Greenburg Owens. Greenburg was born in Kentucky in 1818, and, along with many members of the Owens clan, migrated from Kentucky to the Amarugia area in the 1840's. I do not believe that Basey was Greenburg's father because Greenburg's father, Elias O.

Owens lived until 1873, Basey is said to have passed away prior to 1850. Basey could have been one of Greenburg's uncles, Solomon Owens or Samuel Owens, but I can find no evidence that either of these two men were ever in the area. Remember that King Owens II was noted as a "descendent" of King Owens I, which means that Owens II could be linked in several different ways to Owens I. I can find no obvious link between the two from genealogical records, which doesn't mean there isn't one, just that I have been unable to find it.

Greenburg is one of the few Owens family members that I have found living in the area and passing away in the proper time frames. There is no definitive record of Greenburg's passing, but most records say that he died "prior to 1870. Existing records do confirm that Greenburg lived in the Amarugia area. The 1860 census reports that at this time he and his family lived in the Dolan Township, which borders the Everett Township to the north. Greenburg is the oldest son of Elias O. Owens and Elizabeth who moved their large family from Floyd County, Kentucky, into Cass County, Missouri, between 1840 and 1842. (This timeframe is confirmed by the fact that Elias and Elizabeth's youngest child, Solomon, was born in Kentucky in 1839 and their daughter, Melvina, was married in Cass County in 1842.) The State Historical Society of Missouri's Place Name database says that Owens Creek, the central waterway through Amarugia, was named after Greenbury's father, Elias Owens. (Johnson, 1933) The chart below shows details about the Elias Owens family that likely made the trip from Floyd County, Kentucky to Cass County, Missouri:

Name	Birth/Death	Lived in Cass County?	Burial Location
Greenbury Owens	1818 – prior to 1870	Yes, 1860 Census	Unknown
Thomas Owens	1820 - ?	No, may have died as a child	Unknown
James Owens	1822-1876	Unknown	Unknown
Squire Owens	1822-1876	No	Kentucky
Melvina Owens	1824- 1876	Yes	Fannin, TX
Chederick Shaderick?) Owens	1829 - ?	Yes, 1850 Census	Unknown

Elijah Owens	1831-1890	Yes, 1850 census	Fannin, TX
Major Hickman Owens	1835-1893	Yes, 1850 Census	Fannin, TX
Nancy D Owens	1836-?	Unknown, but likely	Unknown
Solomon Owens	1839- 1900	Yes, 1850 Census	Unknown

Greenburg Owens is also the father of Elias L. Owens, an Everett resident who is mentioned in historical records as being named "Attorney General of the Kingdom of Amarugia" under King David in the 1890s. This tells us that the son, Elias L. Owens, was likely part of the Owens family who was active in leadership of the kingdom.

After issues with the neighboring peoples at the beginning of his reign, King Owens II is said to have brought a period of peace to the area and "for many years the province enjoyed a period of prosperity that was scarcely equaled in the history of any nation." (History, 1949) King Owens II, who ruled for many years, is said to have died after a long reign. This may put the end of his reign in the late 1860s. Making his rule as king to have run somewhere between 1845 and 1870.
<u>Confidence level that Greenburg Owens is King Owens II: 60%</u>

Unfortunately, the time of peace and prosperity would end upon the death of King Owens II. It was determined that his only qualifying descendent was too old and blind which made that person "unfit to steer the ship of state through the waves that threatened it with dissolution." (History, 1949) Due to this lack of a qualified heir, the position of King was opened to the rest of the community and the decision as to who would become the new king was entrusted to a "council of deputies". The members of this council were selected by the "Imperial Council" which had been created under King Owens II.

The council of deputies, after completing their search, named Sir Thomas Bundy as the new king. King Bundy's reign was said to have been prosperous and during most of his reign, his subjects were happy and content. I have not found any indication as to how long King Bundy's reign lasted, but we know that there were a few good years and then things went downhill in the kingdom. King Bundy's problems are said to have been due to political infighting inside the kingdom which eventually resulted in the banishment of King Bundy.

There was a Cass County resident named Thomas Wadkins Bundy who was born in 1842 in Russel, Virginia, and came to Cass County around 1875. Thomas Bundy is listed on the 1880 census as living in Everett Township at that time. Thomas married his wife, Sarah Reynolds Bundy, in 1871, in Sullivan, Tennessee, after which the newlyweds quickly left for Missouri. This is confirmed because their first two children died in childbirth in Missouri. Between 1872 and 1880, the couple would have eight children, only three of which lived. Their son, Lee Roy Bundy, was born in November of 1880, in Vernon County, Missouri, which means that the family had left Cass County prior to his birth. This timeline fits the story, if we assume that Sir Thomas came to Cass County in 1872, became a respected resident in the next couple years and was named king by the Council of Deputies sometime between 1875 and 1877. Legend says that he ruled for only a few successful years but was then banished, which would explain his departure to Vernon County in 1880.

Confidence level that Thomas Wadkins Bundy is King Sir Thomas Bundy: 70%

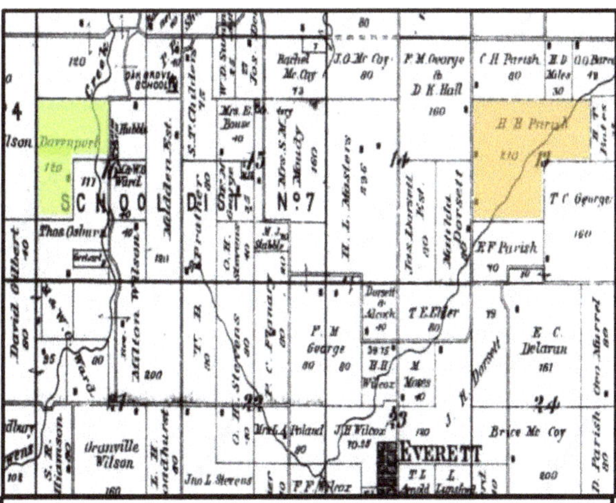

Figure 17: 1895 Everett Township plat map shows the land holdings by Davenport and H.H Parish. I should note that Davenport's holdings do not show his initials so I can't be 100% positive it is J. F. Davenport, but the dates lead me to believe that it is.

The political strife that King Bundy faced was reportedly due to competing factions in the kingdom. The 1949 article says that the two factions were led by a man named Davenport and another named Parish. Neither of these men officially became king. One report infers that Davenport, while never becoming king, did at one point hold the reigns of the government. It is likely that this period is between 1881 and 1884.

The people in the kingdom apparently grew weary of the conflict between the Davenport and Parish factions and at some point, in 1884 or 1885, a man referred to as the Duke of Wellington became the king. The new king immediately established an outreach program with the neighboring "nations" and is said to have brought peace to the land.

It is highly likely that the Duke of Wellington was a man named Jacob Weddington (1837-1916). How Wellington with two "L's" became Weddington with two "D's", I'm not sure. To add more confusion to the question, Jacob Weddington's grave marker in Moudy Cemetery spells the name "Wedington" with only one "D". I can't explain any of these spelling inconsistencies. Are they simply errors or are they possibly due to outdated spellings that were used in one spot and not another? I don't know for sure.

Figure 18: Two images of Jacob Weddington's tombstone located in Moudy Cemetery. The image on the left is from www.findagrave.com and I believe was taken quite some time ago as the letters are much more visible than they are today. The image on the right is from this author's visit in 2024 to the site and the headstone is much worse shape. Note the spelling of the name with only one "D".

In this case, I feel very confident about the identity of this person. This confidence is based on other facts pertaining to Jacob Weddington. Soon after beginning his reign, King Jacob, a Confederate war veteran, attempted to bring peace between the different regions by marrying his son "Count Samuel" to "Princess Clara Garrett". "By this happy alliance . . .peace was forever insured between Amarugia and the warlike tribes of Happy Valley." (History 1947)

The man I believe is the Duke of Wellington, Jacob Weddington, would have been 48 years old when he became king and would have been in Missouri since at least 1870, which is confirmed by the 1870 census. Genealogical records tell us that Mr. Weddington's oldest son, Samuel Weddington (Count Samuel), married a woman named Clara Belle Garrett (Princess Clara) on November 3, 1887, which matches the legend and time-frame perfectly.

In addition to the Royal marriage, legend tells us that King Jacob also sent and received emissaries from the neighboring kingdoms. The "warlike" Kingdom of Happy Valley sent Sir Jno L. Stephens ("Jno" is an old way of writing "John") to Amarugia and in response Amarugia sent Bur McAnally to Happy Valley. Sir Dr. Arnold was sent to Amarugia from the Kingdom of Everett and Sir Jno N. Davidson was sent to Amarugia from "No Man's Land".

This map shows where I believe these other kingdoms were located. This map is created using the plat map of 1895, finding the land owned by these men and then making the assumption that the land they owned was inside the "kingdom" they called home. The size and shape of the other kingdoms is purely a guess, as I have no idea the size each of these other kingdoms.

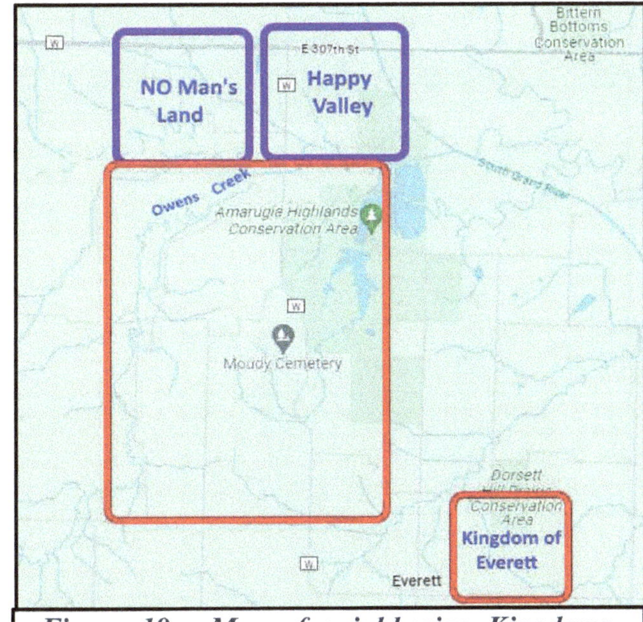

Figure 19: Map of neighboring Kingdoms created based on 1895 land ownership of men sent to Amarugia during the reign of King Weddington. (Courtesy Google Maps)

Confidence level that the Duke of Wellington is Jacob Weddington: 95%

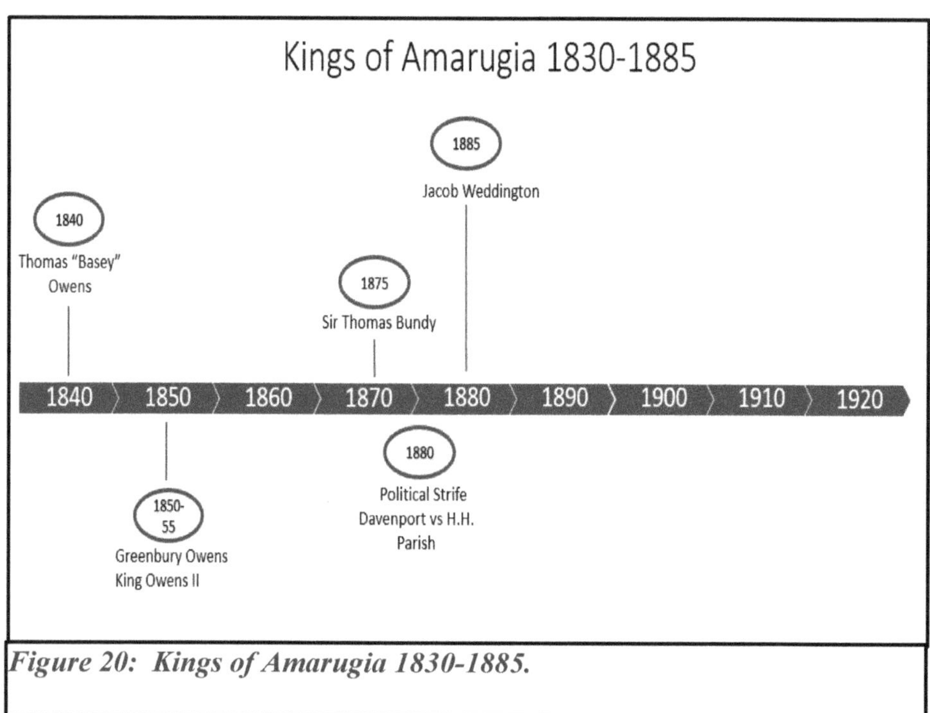

Figure 20: Kings of Amarugia 1830-1885.

The Royal Line Continued

The *Cass County Democrat-Missourian*'s 1949 article calls Sir Thomas Bundy, "one of the first to wear the crown", even though inside the same article they have reprinted the 1887 article, which tells of King Owens I and King Owens II. The article describes Bundy as. . .

…the king, the lord high executioner, and the lord high-everything-else for years. He was a stern ruler, yet just in all his official acts and exercised a great influence over his subjects. In political matters especially.

If you recall, the earlier account told us that King Bundy was banished from the region. The 1949 article softens that by saying that he simply moved away and upon his abdication appointed Jacob Weddington to wear the crown. In his book *The History of Everett*, Ted Davis says that the "Duke of Wellington" (named king prior to Sir Thomas Bundy) and "Jacob Wellington" (named king after Sir Thomas Bundy) are two different people. He could be correct, but my research does not support this finding. I believe that they are, in fact, the same person and the use of the term "Duke of Wellington" is the community embracing the Royal Line idea and using the title of a well-known English aristocrat whose name sounded very much like Jacob Weddington's.

The 1949 article contends that King Jacob Weddington, who was bald and going blind, eventually gave up his crown because, according to the article, the kingdom decided that a bald man could not rule the kingdom unless he agreed to have the crown glued to his bald head. King Jacob refused and if we believe this story, that is what ended his reign.

At this point, all accounts agree that a man named David W. Wilson, fought for, and was named king in or around 1889. It was reported in the 1889 article that "it was an open secret that Admiral Dave Wilson aspires to the throne." The fact that David W. Wilson became the king is in little dispute. In fact, Wilson's tombstone in the Lee's Summit

Cemetery tells the world that he was "The King of Amarugia 1895 - 1913".

Osborn's research found that King David was shot by a "bushwhacker" in his youth which left a hole in the side of his mouth. Due to this injury, his teeth on one side had to be pulled out so that he could get food into his mouth. King David was ambitious and proud of the fact that he was the King of Amarugia. He is remembered as being wealthy and living a life of leisure both as a farmer and a shop owner in Everett. One woman remembered "King David" as a man who acted like he was king of something, but she didn't ever know exactly of what. (Osborn, 17)

King David embraced the role and regularly communicated to his subjects through the local papers. The first written record of King David taking any official action is in the *Cass County Democrat-Missourian* in March of 1894, when he issued a "Royal Proclamation" officially moving the "central seat of our dominion" to Everett, where, not surprisingly, he had just relocated. David also announces who will hold several high-ranking positions in the kingdom for the coming years. (Read the entire Royal Proclamation in the next Chapter.) The proclamation, which was published on March 8, 1894, in the *Cass County Democrat-Missourian*, is signed:

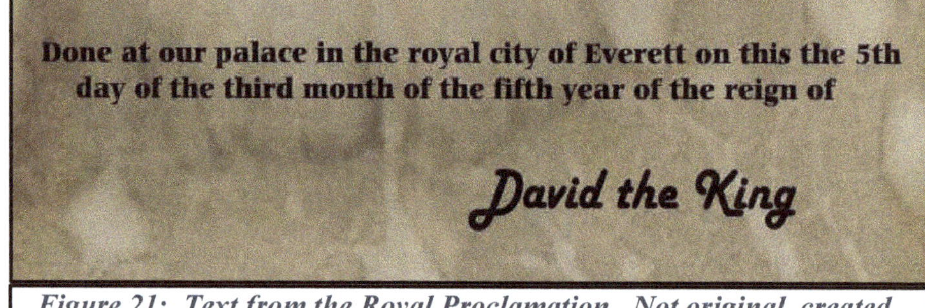

Figure 21: Text from the Royal Proclamation. Not original, created by author for effect.

If we can believe the date and wording on this proclamation, it tells us that King David ascended to the throne around January of 1889. Which would also tell us that the previous king, Jacob Weddington, would have reigned from approximately 1885 – 1889.

The 1895 plat maps show us that at this time, King David was a substantial landowner in the area, owning a very large piece of land in the heart of the kingdom just south of the Grand River and encompassing a significant portion of the northern branch of Owens Creek. Also notice from the maps below that Jacob Weddington, the man who was king prior to Wilson taking the throne, also owned land in the same area. Weddington' s land was almost entirely surrounded by Wilson's land, except to the north.

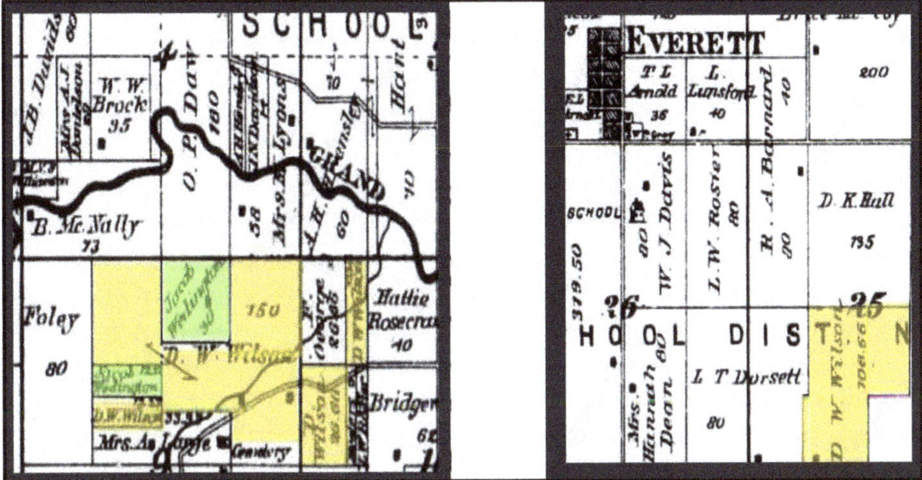

Figure 22 Left: From the 1895 plat Map shows the landholdings both Jacob Wedington (with one "D") and David W Wilson. These holdings are in section 9 which is just southeast of the confluence of Owens Creek and the South Fork of the Grand River. Right: Wilson also owned a large piece of land in Section 25, just southwest of the City of Everett.

The 1949 article tells us that King David got into some "lady" problems which brought his reign to an end. "He [King David] finally got into serious difficulty with some of his female subjects and came near being beheaded by the male population. He gave up the crown and left." (History, 1949) As shown by the maps above, King David was a substantial landowner in the area in 1895, but by the year 1912, his name appears nowhere on the plat maps of Everett Township. David's "lady problems" apparently forced him to liquidate his land holdings and leave the area entirely by 1912. The exact year that King David abdicated the throne is unknown, but a 1911 newspaper column calls David the "ex-King". The "ex-king" moniker leads one to believe that he was gone by 1911. To add more confusion to the days of his reign, his own tombstone put in place after his death in 1933 in Lee's Summit Historical Cemetery, in Lee's Summit, Missouri, notes that he was the king of Amarugia from 1895 – 1913, which appears to remove a few years from the beginning and add a couple years at the end his reign.

David's own Royal Proclamation dated 1894 was signed by David in the fifth year of his reign. Simple math tells us that his reign had begun in 1889, six years before the timeline inscribed on his tombstone. It's worth noting here that King David had no children and his wife, Fannie, preceded him in death by 11 years, passing away in 1922. Gross says in the epilogue to his book that King David's great-nephew, Donald Read, is the person that updated the tombstone - both the date of death, as well as the "King of Amarugia 1895 – 1913" inscription. I don't want to say that Mr. Read put the wrong dates, he may have possessed other information that I don't have, but I believe my dates are correct and are supported by historical artifacts. It would not be surprising if, without the benefit of modern research techniques, the years that were inscribed on the headstone were off just a little.

Figure 23: David W. Wilson, King David. Buried in Lee's Summit Cemetery.

After King David left the area, the 1949 article says that Jacob Weddington was again asked to take over as the king. Legend says that Weddington agreed to serve only if he didn't have to glue the crown to his head. Apparently, the community decided it was okay to have a bald king this time and King Jacob ascended to the throne a second time. The article describes the returning king in this way, "He is one of the oldest settlers in that famous kingdom and is highly respected by all his subjects. He is almost blind, but he is full of fun and is looking at the bright and humorous side of life." (History, 1949)

King Jacob, who has already been discussed as he had already served as the king once prior, was a Confederate Veteran who mustered into the Confederate Army in 1861 at Morristown with the Second

Cavalry. His Confederate pension application, which was filed when he was 78 years old in 1915, lists that he fought at "Springfield, MO, Helena AR, Can Hill AR, Prairie Grove AR and Jefferson City MO". (Pension Document) The image on the next page shows Weddington's (with two "Ds") Confederate pension application from 1915 at which time he was 78 years old. Note the shaky signature on the form. Jacob Weddington would pass away a year after this application was filed in 1916.

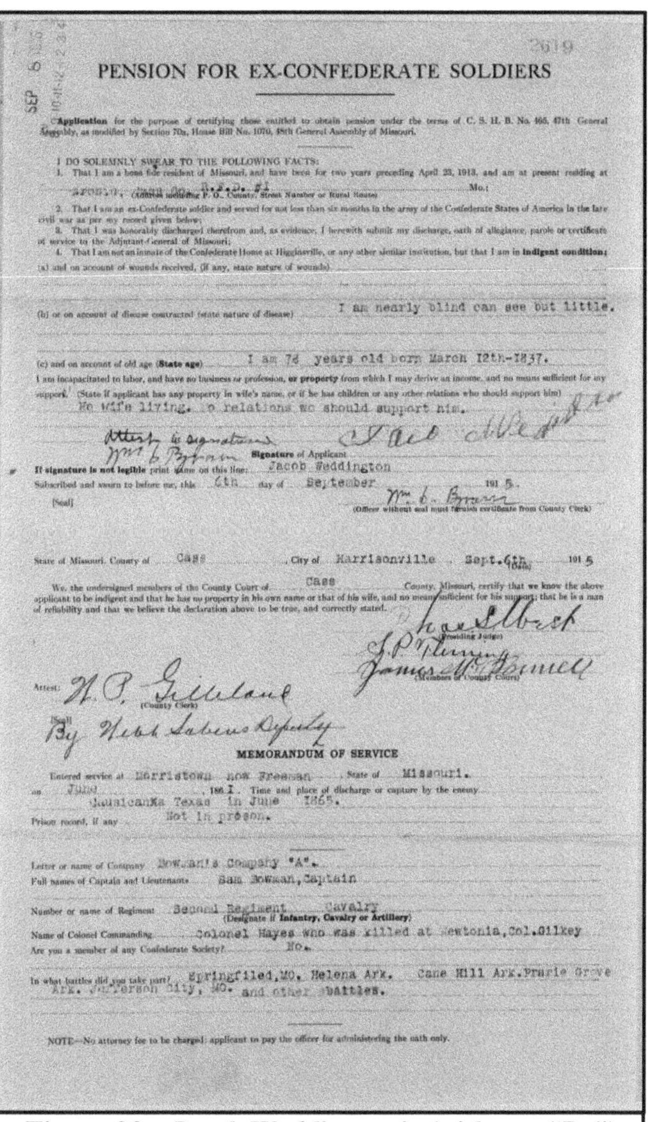

Figure 23: Jacob Weddington's (with two "Ds") Pension application for ex-Confederate soldiers. He would have signed this at 78 years old. He died a year later.

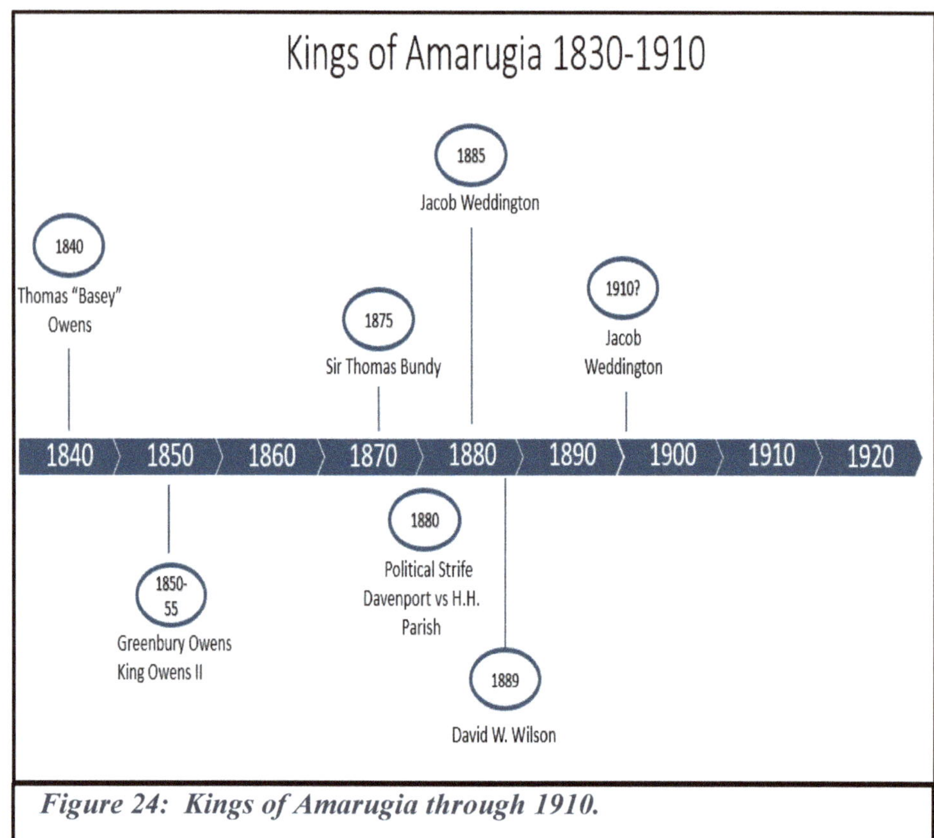

*Figure 24: **Kings of Amarugia through 1910.***

King David's Royal Proclamation

After ascending to the throne in 1889 and ruling for 5 years, King David had this "Royal Proclamation" printed in the *Cass County Democrat-Missourian* on March 8, 1894. The text is very difficult to understand, for that reason, I have broken the text into smaller sections to clarify what is actually being said.

To our Liege and well-beloved Subjects of the Realm of Amaurugia [sp] and the Outlying Provinces, Greeting:

The word "Liege" is an old-time word for "feudal superior". The "Outlying Provinces" are neighboring "nations" to the "Realm of Amarugia". In today's world you might think of multiple neighborhoods that border each other. It is odd in this section that King David or the paper misspelled Amarugia. You would think that is one thing that they would get right!

WHEREAS, -- Our royal pleasure hath led us to select as the central seat of our dominion, the good city of Everett, we hereby notify our loving subjects that all who seek our royal presence may find us there. We further announce our intention to speedily extend our gracious and benign authority over all those more distant regions of our happy realm wherein some of the misguided and benighted persons have heretofore failed to render due obedience to our benignant sway.

King David is moving to Everett, so he is moving the seat of the kingdom to that city. Anyone who wants to deal with the Kingdom of Amarugia will find him there. He also announces in this passage that he is expanding Amarugia, and thus his span of control, to include the "outlying provinces". He calls out certain persons in those neighboring regions as "misguided and benighted". Benighted is defined as "in a state of pitiful intellectual or moral ignorance". The last sentence basically means that the persons should immediately begin to obey and take advantage of the "benignant" or kind and generous nature of the King.

If there be yet therein, any whose malignant hearts nourish the noxious seeds of rebellion against our mild rule, we warn them that only speedy submission can avert our just anger; the coyote must take to the brush when the lion comes down from the mountain.

In this passage the king is saying that if you oppose the King of Amarugia taking over a wider swath of territory, we will hunt you down and make sure you submit to our rules. He is comparing these "malignant hearts who nourish the noxious seeds of rebellion" to the coyote who must hide in the bushes when the lion (the kingdom) comes to get them.

And whereas, our realm hath now become so wide extended and POPULOUS that we may not give our personal attention to the details of the public business; in order that the same may never be neglected to the injury of our subjects and the scandal of our rule, it pleaseth us to appoint Jerry Dorsett and Brice McCoy our Chief Advisers and Speakers of our sovereign pleasure, well knowing that in a multitude of words there must needs be some wisdom.

Because the kingdom is now larger, King David needs to appoint helpers to assist in taking care of the duties of running the kingdom. The next two paragraphs simply make those assignments. Of special note in this section is the appointment of Jerry Dorsett as "Chief Adviser and Speaker of our sovereign pleasure". Mr. Dorsett is later identified as a man who served as king in the later days of the kingdom. Jeremiah (Jerry) Dorsett would also go on to serve a single term in the Missouri House of Representatives. This role of "advisor and speaker" is likely that of a spokesman or negotiator.

We constitute our well-beloved subject and dutiful adherent, John George, our Lord High Treasurer and Chief Almoner of our Largess. At the gate of entrance, in the Northwest Province,

we place Joel Henry and B.W. McAnally as Surveyors of Customs. In the Northeastern Province of this, our realm of Amauragia [sp], we designate W. H. Steen and Reuben Todd, and in the Western Province thereof, James W. Bishop and J.R. Watson our High Muck-a-Mucks; granting to them full authority to maintain order therein as the representatives of our august person, and we do commend to them that mild and gentle manner of government, which hath made our Kingdom the envy of its less fortunate neighbors;

Another paragraph of appointments. I'm going to highlight and define a few of these roles and explain what I believe the job entailed since the language is outdated and difficult to understand. The **Chief Almoner of Our Largess**, a title for which I had to look up both words, is the person who is responsible for giving to charity. The **Surveyors of Customs** is likely someone who is responsible for people and goods coming in and out of the area. The **High Muck-a-Mucks** are responsible for enforcement of rules. The term "our august person" means a person who is inspiring and deserves reverence. It appears that David is talking about himself here. King David seems to be a little full of himself.

. . . nevertheless, we do strictly command them to be at all time a holy terror to evil dowers, and should the peace of those ever smiling Provinces be disturbed by stiff-necked and rebellious maligners of our royal self and slanderers of our good subjects and liegemen, we do empower and instruct our said High Muck-a-mucks to inflict upon each of such graceless offenders and baseborn varlets, the Bastinado, morning, noon and night, daily for calendar month.

This is a massive run on sentence for those English majors out there. King David is saying that all subjects should work to remove "evil doers", also referred to as, "rebellious maligners". The "evil doers" may say bad things about our subjects and liegemen. Liegemen is just another name for "loyal subjects", which makes the use of "subjects and liegemen" a bit redundant. David then continues to say that the Muck-a-mucks are empowered to punish these "graceless offenders and varlets".

Varlets is simply another name for a rascal or rogue. The prescribed punishment for these varlets is the process of bastinado inflicted upon them "morning, noon, and night for a month.   Bastinado is a punishment, which is still used in certain countries of the Middle East and Asia. The person being punished has their feet tied together and the soles of their feet were whipped with a stick or flogged with a coarse rope.   The proclamation recommends that violators, or "graceless offenders and baseborn varlets", be punished using this method three times a day for a calendar month.

Figure 25: Bastinado, a punishment that involves flogging of the feet.

The City of Everett, the "Central Seat of our Dominion"

The Everett, Missouri, post office was established in 1857. It took another 10 years before the land in the city of Everett, Missouri was platted in 1867. Per the 1912 plat map, the town was located on the northwest side of the intersection of Route W (E 339 St) and S Dorsett Hill Rd. (see map below)

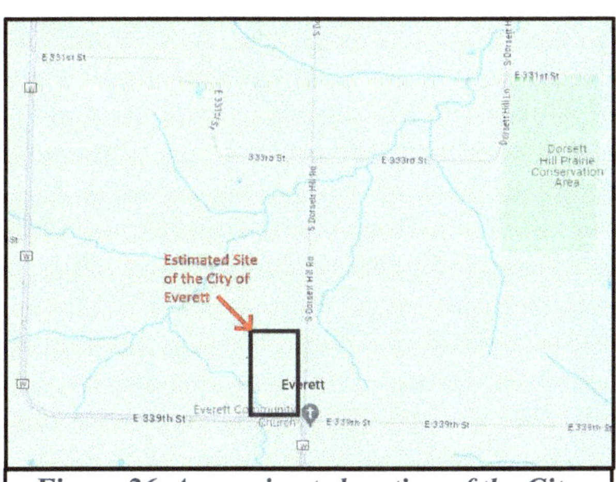

Figure 26 Approximate location of the City of Everett. Nothing remains of the city today. (Courtesy Google Maps)

Cass County, renamed from Van Buren to Cass in 1849, was created in 1837 and it is assumed that Everett Township was created at the same time. Real estate records date back as far as 1840. This fact is important to the story because the name of the city of Everett is commonly attributed to a man named Edward Everett. Could the town and the township be named after the same man, albeit 20 years later? Possibly. Edward Everett was well-known in the United States from around 1830-1860. He was a politician, a Unitarian Pastor, an educator, the 15th governor of Massachusetts and the United States Secretary of State. His tenure as Secretary of State was very short. He only served in this capacity for 5 months after being appointed by President Millard Fillmore in 1852 to finish out the lame duck term of the previous Secretary of State who had passed away. In 1836, when the township was created, Everett was the Governor of Massachusetts, but he was well-known across the nation for his work as a Unitarian pastor.

Everett served as Massachusetts Governor from 1836 – 1840, as Minister to the United Kingdom from 1841-1845, and as President of Harvard University from 1846-1848. After his short stint as Secretary of State, he ran for and was elected to the United States Senate where he only served one year from 1853 – 1854. In 1854, after some rough political sledding, Everett resigned his seat in the U.S. Senate citing health reasons.

Figure 28: Edward Everett, Pastor, and Politician.

Edward Everett throughout his career was always a man who supported the preservation of the Union. He was generally anti-slavery and opposed allowing slavery in the new western states. However, he was concerned that more radical "anti-slavery" groups and their ideals would eventually tear the union apart. He did not support the Kansas/Nebraska Act, in 1854 for much the same reason. Around the time the city of Everett was formed and leading up to the Civil War, he was a national voice for the preservation of the Union and a harsh critic of John Brown's tactics in Kansas. For these views, it is entirely possible that the mostly pro-southern residents of Everett Township also decided to name their town after Senator Everett. Of course, another option is that since the township was named Everett, the town in that zone should also be named Everett.

The plat Map of 1877 shows that the city of Everett consisted of 8 blocks with a street running north/south between the east and west sides. By 1885, the official plat shows that the city had been

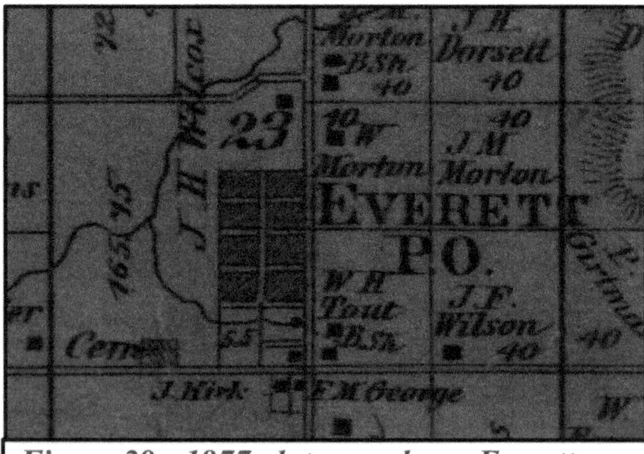

Figure 29: 1877 plat map shows Everett consisting of 8 blocks.

extended to include 10 lots, with 5 side by side lots with two other lots extending to the south on the eastern side. The city always had one main street running down the center and the town was bordered on the

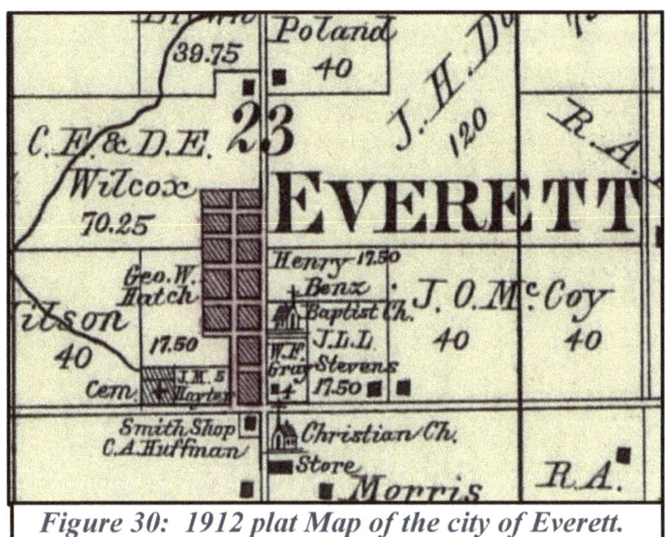

Figure 30: 1912 plat Map of the city of Everett.

eastside by what is now S Dorsett Hill Road. The two southernmost lots appear in the 1895 and 1912 maps and are labeled as "D.H. Stratton Addition" and "Willet & Johnson's Addition". These lots were likely added at some point to account for future growth. Growth that would never come.

The *1883 History of Cass County* lists the Everett business community as including the following enterprises:

E. I. Arnold,	Physician
J. P. Akers,	Saloon Owner
D. S. and J. R. Brown,	Carpenters
L. T. Dorsett,	Postmaster
Dorsett & Parrish,	Retail Store
Charles Huffman,	Blacksmith
W. H. Lout,	Physician
Locke and Son,	Retail Store
J. N. Morton,	Blacksmith
W. H. Reucupohl,	Blacksmith
Mrs. H. Scott, and daughter,	Milliners (a "milliner" sells women's hats)
Robert Wilson,	Blacksmith

Six years later in 1889, according to Ted Davis's *History of Everett*, the town of Everett was thriving and growing larger. The small town now boasted a barber shop, a weaver, several lawyers, two carpenter shops, a dressmaker, a storekeeper with only one clerk, an ax handle maker, two blacksmith shops, three churches; Methodist, Christian and Baptist Church, and a single bar called the Main City Tavern. (Davis, 22)

King David announced that the center of the Kingdom of Amarugia was the city of Everett in his Royal Proclamation in March of 1894. David likely made this change because he had moved to the city of Everett at this time. King David had several land holdings in the area, therefore, it is not possible to know exactly where he was living at this time. In an interview with the Kansas City Star, Osborn remembers visiting the rotting frame of King David's home, which was in Everett. This confirms that King David did live in Everett at one point. (Gupta)

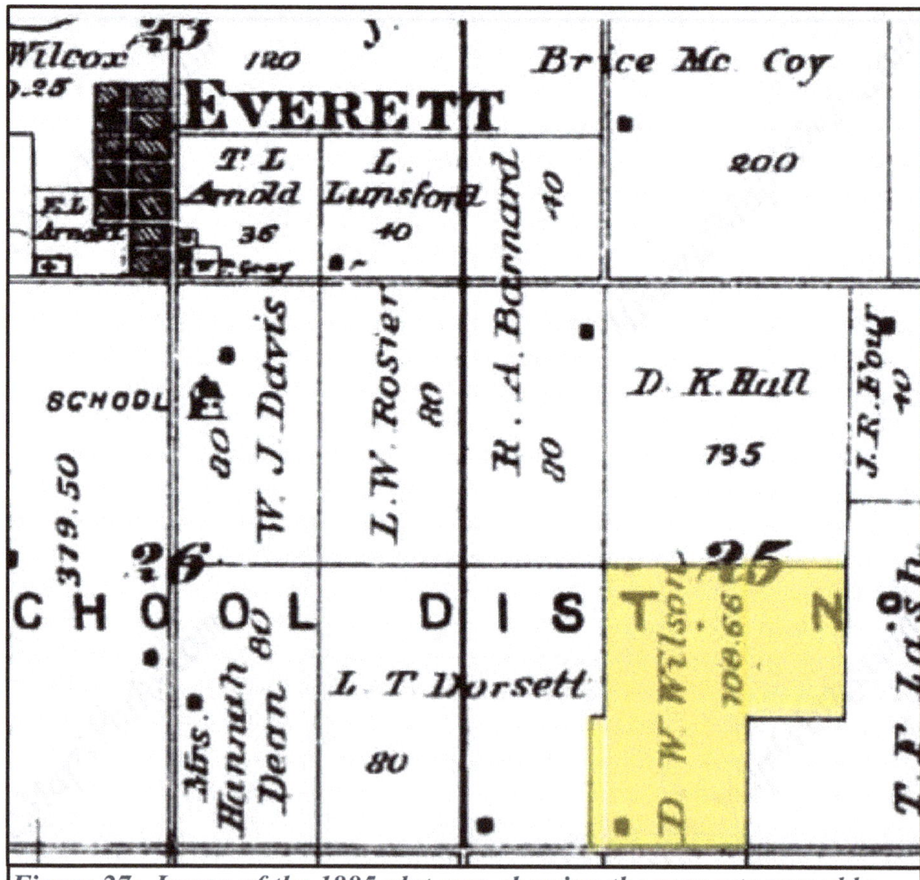

Figure 27: Image of the 1885 plat map showing the property owned by David Wilson located southeast of the city of Everett.

The growth reported in 1889 seemed to fizzle out quickly as the plat map for 1895, only six years later, shows very few lots in the town having owners. The final blow came in 1906 when the Everett Post Office closed. In fact, *The History and Directory of Cass County, Missouri*, published by the *Cass County Leader* in 1908, reported zero residents living in the city of Everett at that time.

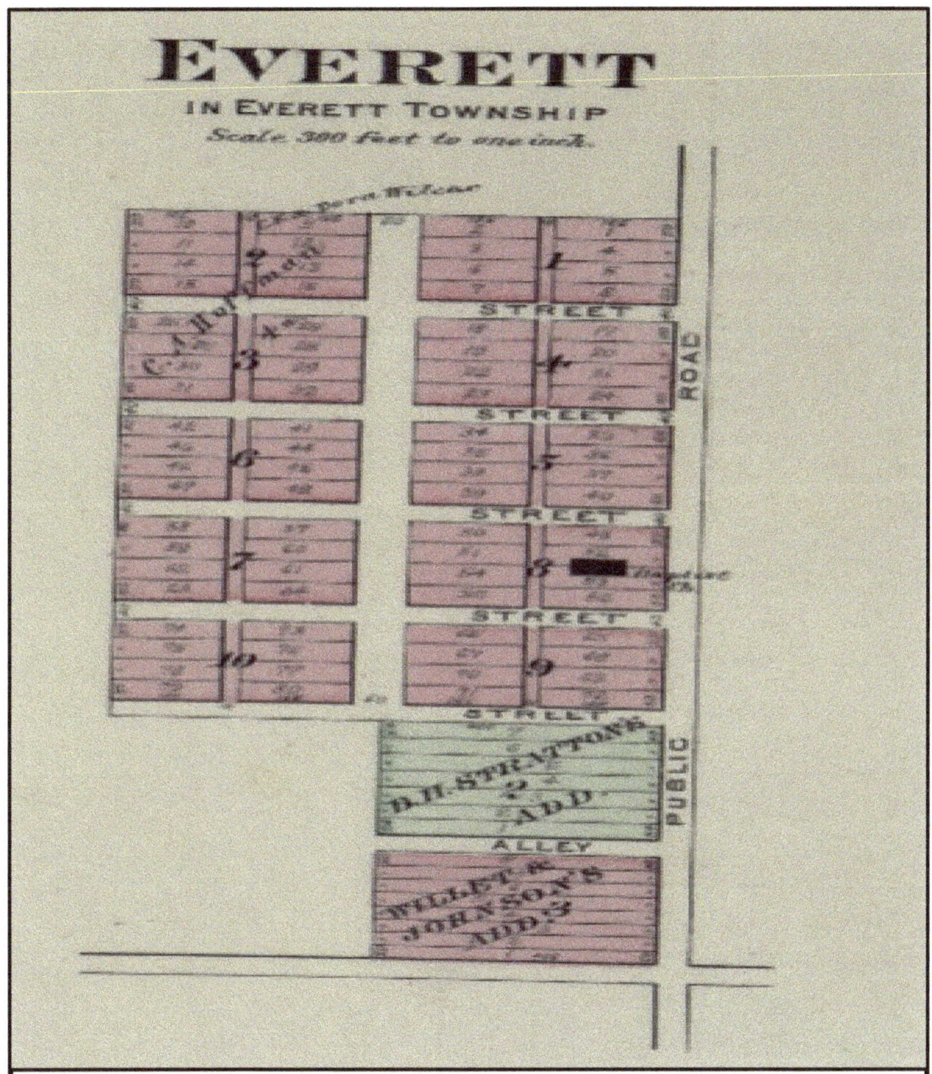

Figure 28: 1912 plat showing the layout of the city of Everett. This map also shows the lack of ownership of most of the lots that once made up the city.

Today the only remnant of the town of Everett is the Christian Church, now the Everett Community Church, (which can be seen in the 1912 plat map, figure 33) which is still located diagonally across the intersection southwest from where the town once stood. The satellite image below shows the site where the town once stood. Current landowners have told me that there is absolutely no evidence on the property that a town ever existed at this location.

Figure 29: The red box shows the former location of the town of Everett. (Courtesy of Google Maps)

Life in Amarugia

Daily life in Amarugia was not much different than it was anywhere else on the western frontier, except for the fact that its residents were ruled by a king. Life in the kingdom evolved over time and as would be expected, was much different during the reign of Kings Owens I and II than it was when King David ruled in the latter part of the 19th century. To better explain these differences, this chapter will be divided into two sections: one from the 1840s through 1875, and another from 1875 through 1910. Very little documentation exists for the earlier period, for that reason, I have relied on historical resources to tell what life may have been like in rural Missouri in the early and mid-1800s.

Life in Amarugia under King Owens and King Owens II. (1840-1875)

King Owens I came to Amarugia around 1837 as a fur trader. In the early years the community would have been made up mainly of men who trapped and traded furs with the local Osage Indians and with the U. S. Government. Much of this trading would have taken place at Fort Osage on the Missouri River, just north of the present-day Buckner, Missouri, around 55 miles to the north. Most of the furs traded on the western frontier at this time would have passed through Fort Osage which was a major commerce point at the time. Those not willing or able to make the journey to Fort Osage would likely have been able to sell their furs, for a lesser price, at the local trading post run by Basey Owens on what is now known as Owens Creek.

In the early days of Cass County and Amarugia, furs would have been plentiful and life as a fur trader would have been good. As time passed and more people migrated to the area, the area was over-trapped, and furs would have become harder to come by. This would have made making a living as a trapper much more difficult.

Seeing and interacting with Native Americans would have been common during this early period. While the Osage Indians were likely the most common Native Americans seen in the Amarugia area, other tribes were also present including the Kansa, Omaha, Quapaw and Ponca tribes. While records are scarce, the Cass County Historical Society says that while times were difficult for the residents, "At no

Figure 30:   Trading Post location taken from Robert L. Gross, "Amarugia", page 4. (Courtesy Google Maps)

time were the early settlers in particular danger from the Indians". (www.CassCounty.com) Most accounts lead us to believe that the Native Americans in the area were nomadic and did not maintain permanent settlements in the Amarugia or Cass County area. The Natives in the area during these times were likely traveling through to hunt or to trade with the existing residents or government entities.

Lodging for the settlers of this time were log cabins. The earlier cabins, built for male residents, would have been small and built to simply provide a roof over their head and a warm place to sleep. As more women came to the area, the cabins would have gotten larger with more luxuries if the homeowner had the means to acquire

Figure 31: Sharp-Hopper log cabin. Built in Northern Cass County in 1835 and moved to the Harrisonville Library in 1976.

those niceties. The Sharp-Hopper log cabin, built in 1835 in northern Cass County, is an example of a cabin of the time and can be seen at the Cass County Library in Harrisonville. It is a large cabin for its time and was likely owned by a relatively wealthy family.

During the frontier days in Amarugia, one of the main social gatherings was the Brush Arbor Revival. These religious meetings were held in towns and villages large and small across the county. The small town of Everett was known to have hosted these "camp meetings". The meetings would last for several days with different preachers taking turns speaking to the crowd. Traveling preachers would make it known to area residents that they would be in the area on certain dates and plans for a revival would get underway. This advanced notice gave the locals time to clear a spot large enough for the expected crowds, construct the brush arbor, and cut logs for seating under the arbor. (Scott, 1975).

These camp meetings or revivals were a big social event in the area as it was one of the few times that residents

Figure 32: Not from Amarugia, but a good example of a Brush Arbor.

from across the entire area would gather. The revivals, while certainly serving a religious purpose to the residents, were also important to the community for the social aspect of the gathering. These events were truly a family occasion, where upon arrival the women would gather with the other women, the men with the men and the older children would find their own space to be together. If the location of the meeting was convenient to their homes, families would go home for the night and return in the morning. If the distance back home was too far, families would set up camp near the meeting location and spend multiple days at the event without going home.

These meetings were also events that the Native Americans were said to enjoy immensely. It is said that the Natives enjoyed the overall atmosphere of the events, particularly the singing and revelry that accompanied a brush arbor meeting. They may have attended for faith purposes also as the Native Americans of that time were certainly exposed to religion by the white settlers coming to the region. Large numbers of Native Americans were converting to Christianity during this time. On their website, the Cass County Historical Society tells of as many as 500 Native Americans attending a religious camp meeting held by white settlers in the area southwest of Harrisonville, not far from Amarugia.

In his book, Robert Gross says that different people with different backgrounds responded to different types of preaching. The Prairie people, northerners mainly from Ohio, Illinois, and Indiana, tended to prefer the more laid-back soft-spoken ministers, while Amarugians from the highlands, southerners from Kentucky, Tennessee, and western North Carolina, preferred the fire and brimstone, Bible thumping orators. (Gross, 91) It should be noted that Gross's book is a work of fiction, but the stories are based on local stories of the area during this time.

Another gathering that was a little less merry, was Saturday morning court which was reportedly held each Saturday morning at 9 am. The residents of the kingdom would gather, and the king would listen to both sides of an issue and then make a ruling as to the penalty or the punishment. Fines were usually levied in goods, such as pumpkins, good cider, or a few twists of tobacco. (Reeves, 17)

The concept of Saturday morning justice is common to most accounts of the kingdom. It is interesting to note that the kingdom existed and was expected to abide by regular Missouri state laws. However, folklore contends that the people in the kingdom trusted the king to meet out fair and reasonable justice rather than going to the "real authorities" such as the Cass County Sheriff. *Kansas City Star* writer Donald Bradley thinks that justice may have gone a bit further when he says, "Folklore has the king holding Saturday trials for rule breakers and the guilty were hanged. (Bradley, 5/14/2005)

I'm skeptical of the idea that the king had the power to order someone to be hanged. I would reemphasize that Amarugia was still part of Cass County, part of the state of Missouri and part of the United States of America and as part of those regulatory bodies, was expected to follow the laws of those organizations. To think that the king, essentially a non-elected leader, could simply ignore the established courts and law enforcement of the day seems illogical. Handling petty offenses like stealing makes a bit more sense as the Sheriff probably did not make his way out to Amarugia often and appreciated someone keeping the peace without his presence being required.

Figure 33: *Image of a Charivaris.*

On a brighter note, another custom in the early days of the kingdom was the practice of holding charivaris for happy events such as weddings. A "charivaris" is defined as a "noisy mock serenade performed by a group of people to celebrate a marriage or mock an unpopular person." The practice often included yelling, ringing bells, and banging of pots and pans or anything that could be used to make loud noises. This practice is the genesis of the American custom of tying cans to the cars of newlyweds when they leave the ceremony after their betrothal.

The American Civil War was not a pleasant time to be in either Cass County, or in Amarugia. The war occurred during what was likely the reign of King Owens II. Amarugia, like most of the areas on the Missouri/Kansas border, was likely populated by a mixture of southern and northern sympathizers. It is also likely, although there are no numbers to prove this definitively, that a larger number of the residents were southern sympathizers as this would have been true for most of Cass County in 1860. Amarugians would have been impacted by both Bleeding Kansas, and the Civil War, which meant that for all intents and purposes, the residents of Amarugia lived in war like conditions from 1857 through the end of the war in 1865.

While most of the residents may have been pro-southern, Osborn calls out the fact that there seemed to be a small group of northern sympathizers concentrated in the "prairie". This is no surprise considering that the Prairie people, who lived south and east of Dragoon's Trace, were largely from Indiana, Illinois, and Ohio, all northern leaning states. Conversely, the occupants of the highlands, north and west of the trace, were largely from southern leaning states like Kentucky, Tennessee, and North Carolina. It is likely that the bad blood between the two areas was only made worse by the tensions that came with their differing views on the issues causing the civil war. (Osborn, 8)

During this period, Amarugia residents would have dealt with Jayhawkers from the Kansas side and Bushwhackers from the Missouri side riding through the area and creating havoc for the residents. The partisan raiders often did not particularly care about the homeowners' political views, they just wanted to create havoc. In a 1994 article, the *St. Louis Post-Dispatch* says that "the people got fed up with Bushwhackers and Jayhawkers and made it clear that they were not welcome there. This is when they created the Kingdom." (St. Louis, 1994) This is wrong on multiple counts. First, the kingdom had existed since around 1840, well before hostilities relating to the Civil War began. Secondly, Jayhawkers were not welcome anywhere in Missouri as they targeted Missourians, regardless of their political views.

Interestingly, most written accounts of the kingdom seem to blame all the misdeeds during the war on the "Bushwhackers". I think this is semantics and in fact the term Bushwhacker is used as a catch-all term for anyone raiding a farm or homestead. So, in these accounts, the term would include both Missouri Bushwhackers and Kansas Jayhawkers. I point this out because I believe that it would have been much more common for an Amarugian to have been preyed upon by a group of Jayhawkers, who roamed the area leaving a trail of destruction from the beginning of the war through Order Number 11, which we will touch on a little bit later. The website www.civilwaronthewesternborder.org, defines the men who rode with the Jayhawker regiments this way:

Some men who enlisted in the jayhawker outfits were sincere abolitionists, some were devout Unionists and brave soldiers defending their homeland, and others were bullies and thieves who took advantage of the chaos of war. Many who served in the jayhawker brigades and regiments had old scores to settle with proslavery Missourians from the days of Bleeding Kansas.

Don't misunderstand me, there is no doubt that the southern leaning Bushwhackers would have also done their share of damage to the area, but the preponderance of damage was likely done by Jayhawker units.

Jayhawkers were Union Army volunteers, who rode under General James Lane. Lane was both a General and U. S. Senator from the state of Kansas. For Lane, the purpose of the Jayhawker units was to punish Missourians for their actions during the Bleeding Kansas era by stealing and destroying as much Missouri property as they could without having to fight in pitched battles. Since there were no regular Confederate forces in western Missouri through most of the war, it was easy pickings for these units. The reason most men joined the "volunteer" units was due to the lack

Figure 38: U.S. Senator and General James Lane. Leader of the Jayhawkers.

of discipline and the chance for personal gain that came with being a member of these units.

The only defense for southern leaning residents against the Jayhawkers was to hope that the small Bushwhacker groups, led by men such as William Quantrill, Bloody Bill Anderson, and Frank James, would drive the Jayhawker units away before their homes were robbed, damaged, or destroyed. In the beginning of the war, the Bushwhacker groups acted like a neighborhood watch group in the area. They would try to dissuade Jayhawker regiments from damaging and stealing Missouri property. The neighborhood watch concept was in place for most of the first half of the war until August 21, 1863, when William Quantrill and around 300 Bushwhackers raided Lawrence, Kansas, killing around 180 men and boys and destroying a significant part of the city.

Figure 39: Left: William Quantrill. Right: Bloody Bill Anderson. Missouri Bushwhackers.

The raid on Lawrence and the public outcry against it, forced government leaders to take action to get the bushwhackers, or Missouri guerrilla units under control. With this goal in mind, James Lane convinced Union General Thomas Ewing to issue Order Number 11. Order Number 11 was called by historian Thomas Goodrich, "The harshest act of the U.S. Government against its own people in American History." The order basically said that all persons in the rural parts of Jackson, Cass, and Bates County had to leave their homes by September 15th, 1863. If residents agreed to swear an oath to the Union, they would be allowed to live in one of the Union posts. These posts were located in Harrisonville, Pleasant Hill, Independence, and Kansas City. If residents were not living in one of these posts, they were expected to leave the area immediately.

The order hit Amarugia and the rest of Cass County hard. The people simply had to pack up anything they could carry and get out of the county. Most of the residents did not have any horses or mules left as the Jayhawkers and Bushwhackers had taken all but the old and feeble livestock. This meant that "what they could carry", truly meant "what they could carry on their backs". Once the people left their property, there was no expectation that their homes or possessions left behind would still be there, if and when, they were able to return. Some were lucky enough to have relatives outside the Order Number 11 area with whom they could go and stay. Many others left their homes with no idea of where they were going or how to survive once they got there. They just knew that they had to leave the county. Order 11 was a brutal order and many people died on their journey out of the county.

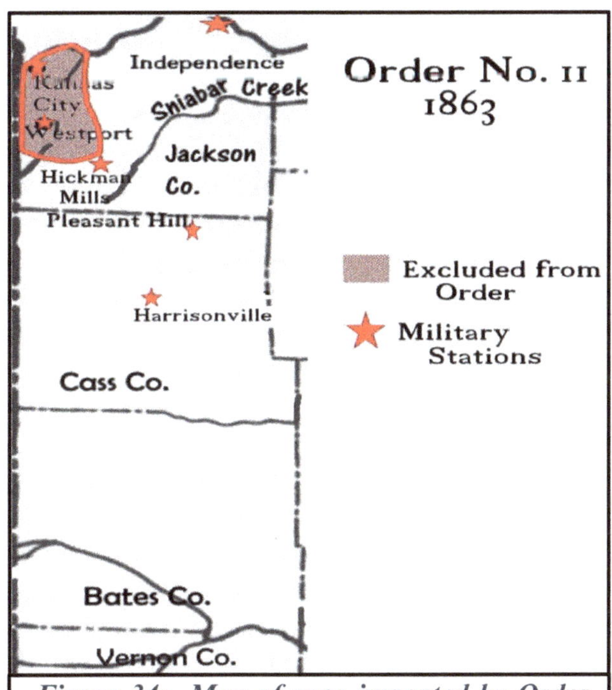

Figure 34: Map of area impacted by Order Number 11. Red Stars denote Military Stations where Union loyalists were allowed to go. The rest of the area had to be vacated.

Some Amarugia residents went to the military posts. One such story involves the Shipley family. The family had come to Amarugia from Tennessee and when the war started, the patriarch of the family, William

Shipley, enlisted to fight for the Confederacy. This left his wife, Amanda, and their four children at home in Amarugia. When Order Number 11 was announced, one of the Shipley son's, Uriah, who was 14 years old, left to fight for the Union Army. (Osborn, 5) Uriah's full name was Uriah McCaleb Shipley, and it appears that many in the family referred to him as "Mack" rather than Uriah.

Order Number 11 forced Amanda and her three remaining children to relocate to Harrisonville. Soon after their arrival, the oldest son still with the family, Preston, started getting into fights with northern sympathizers in town. Family history says that Amanda sent Preston, who was 12 at the time, to stay with future outlaws Cole Younger and Jesse James so they could take care of him until the war was over. Unfortunately, or maybe not, when Cole and Jesse learned how old Preston was, they determined that he was too young to ride with them and sent him to live with a southern family in Peculiar, Missouri.

The timing of this part of the story is a bit suspect. Jesse James himself would have only just turned 16 at the time of Order Number 11. Frank James and Cole Younger would

Figure 35: Left; Jesse, 25, and Frank James, 29. Right: Cole Younger, age unknown, probably about 20–22.

have been riding with Quantrill's Bushwhackers at the time, but Jesse did not ride with them until later the next year. There was a significant Younger family presence in the area and it is possible that Preston was sent to stay with another member of the family or that Cole simply played a part in placing young Preston with another family in the Raymore area. Several sources contend that members of the post-Civil War, James Gang, including Cole Younger and Jesse James, regularly stopped in the Amarugia area to trade horses after the war. (Reeves, 17)

Legend says that the outlaws stopped at the Davenport farm which was located at the base of what is now known as Christenson's Mound (see figure 12). This story is likely true as the James Gang would have been all over western Missouri during their criminal careers.

A Shipley family member interviewed by Osborn also tells a story about their grandfather, William P. Wilson, who at age 74 was too old to join the Confederate Army that he so strongly supported. The story goes that Grandfather Wilson was called out onto his porch one evening and shot dead by a neighbor who reportedly disagreed with his view on the war. Sources confirm that William Wilson did die on April 15, 1864, putting his death during the Civil War.

Another such incident occurred when 17-year-old William P. Sims, who is buried in the Moudy Cemetery was shot and killed by a "bushwhacker" on August 20, 1861, while sitting on a fencepost near his home. Yet another story tells of a night visit made to Elias Moudy, the namesake of the Moudy Cemetery. Moudy was reportedly awakened in the dead of the night by friends and told to leave because the Bushwhackers were coming for him. These incidents show the danger of living in the area during the Civil War. (Osborn, 12)

When the war ended, William Shipley returned home to find that his wife Amanda had passed away from disease after being thrown in jail for singing Confederate songs. It is not clear what became of the rest of the family, but it is very possible that William may have lost the farm in Amarugia when he returned home. This is because northern politicians had made it difficult for ex-Confederate soldiers or southern sympathizers to keep their homes after the war by requiring payment of back taxes on that property. For this reason, it is likely and, in fact, probable, that there was a significant turnover of residents in Amarugia after the war ended.

We know through census records that William Shipley was living in Texas 13 years later. We also know that sometime between 1880 and 1900, William and Amanda's son Preston, returned with his wife, Sarah and their three children and purchased the farm where William and Amanda had lived prior to the war. (McClellan)

Osborn tells another story about a man named Alexander W. (Whit) Cecil who lived in Amarugia with his wife Mary Frost. The story goes that sometime after the Civil War, Whit was working with a "black boy" that was living with him. Whit got angry at the boy and threw a piece of wood at him. The wood hit the "negro" in the head and killed him. Whit was reportedly very upset and wanted to bury the young man in the Everett Cemetery. Unfortunately, the rest of the community would not allow a "negro" to be interred in the cemetery and Whit's request was denied. Instead, Whit and his wife were said to have buried the young man on their property, "on the slope of hill, west of a little draw". (Osborn, 7)

Figure 36: Preston and Sarah Shipley. Preston is the son of Amanda and William Shipley. Preston and his wife Sarah returned to Amarugia and purchased the family home in the late 1800s.

Life in Amarugia under Kings Bundy, Weddington, and Wilson (1875-1910)

Life in the kingdom was probably pretty good during this time frame. As we learned in a previous chapter, the City of Everett, which had been platted in 1867, was growing and bustling by the year 1889. This would lead us to assume that since businesses were thriving, so were the residents of the area, some of which undoubtedly owned and operated those businesses located in Everett.

It is in this time in history that the *Cass County Democrat-Missourian* began to notice Everett and Amarugia. We know some of what was happening in the kingdom because those events are referenced in old copies of the paper. In May of 1886, *The Cass County Democrat* reported that "Amarugia boasts of having the most pretty girls in the country, but the north valley of South Fork produces the prettiest if not the most girls on earth." (Pretty Girls, 5/1886) This seems a bit of an odd statement for a paper to make. They would probably get in trouble for this opinion today.

While the paper did run a regular column for the area, the reality is that there was not much going on. "News is Scarce" is a common theme that can be found in the "Amarugia Headlight" or the "Everett Items" column. The list below shows a sampling of items from those columns from 1889 through 1890.

<u>"Everett Items": February 7, 1889</u> (Osborn, 14-15)
- J. H. Dorsett says he won't go to work in his silver mine till the weather gets warmer.
- Jerry Dorsett is afflicted with the toothache and can't get anything to relieve it.
- Our little town of Everett starts out in the year 1889 well-fortified. Two blacksmith shops, two carpenter shops, one ax handle maker, one storekeeper with one clerk; one barber shop, one doctor, one dressmaker, one weaver; lawyers innumerable; two church houses - - one Baptist and one Methodist.
- Dr. Arnold is also on the sick list, but he still tips the scales at 230.

<u>Amarugia Headlight</u> (*Cass County Democrat-Missourian*: March 20, 1890)

- News is scarce this week.
- King David, the enterprising farmer, and stock dealer of Amarugia has just finished a new addition to one of his farmhouses. King David says, "there is just two things he likes – one is lots of room and the other is just a little more room."
- Someone saw King Henry of No Man's Land racking through our kingdom Sunday. We wonder if he wasn't going to see Ora, the Queen of new Jerusalem?

<u>Amarugia Headlight</u>: (*Cass County Democrat-Missourian*, April 10, 1890)

- King David, the enterprising farmer, and stock dealer of Amarugia is improving his residence and its surroundings considerable this spring. We hope he may live long and prosper.

<u>Amarugia Headlight</u>: (*Cass County Democrat-Missourian*, April 24, 1890)

- News generally scarce in our neighborhood
- Farmers all done sowing flax and some of them are planting corn.
- Our honorable and worthy King, David, was over in the neighborhood of Lone Tree last week buying hogs and cattle, and also took in the circus at schoolhouse No. 1. He says it was superfine.

<u>Amarugia Pickups</u>: *Cass County Democrat-Missourian*, June 5, 1890

- News generally scarce this week
- We would like to know the whereabouts of our benevolent friend, "Sawbuck". He has been missing for some time. We are afraid he has gone up Salt River to return no more.   [Salt River is a tributary of the Mississippi]

It is often mentioned in written stories about Amarugia that no one is willing to admit that they lived in the Kingdom of Amarugia. I find that to not be entirely true as there are many instances of residents of the time who were proud to be living in the kingdom. These persons were also willing to fight anyone who spoke ill of Amarugia.

One such instance can be seen in the story of Frank Hankins, which was originally published in the May 31, 1900, edition of the *Cass County Democrat-Missourian*. A central tenet of the article, titled "A Military Wedding; The 'King of Amarugia' Takes Unto Himself a Bride", is that Frank Hankins was the king of Amarugia. I'll tell the story first and then follow that with the response from Amarugia. The writer refers to the title of King of Amarugia as "a term usually applied in derision in the southwest portion of Cass County." The story goes on to tell the common story of a young man, who convinced an even younger girl, Miss Maud Little, to give into his carnal desires.

Maud, like many girls before her, in a similar situation, assumed that Frank would do the right thing and make an honest woman of her. Unfortunately, Frank had different ideas and despite Maud's pleadings would not agree to the marriage. Eventually, Maud, whose father was away in Dakota, began to show. The article continues the story:

Her secret could no longer be concealed from the eyes of friends, but she bore her shame in silence, hoping that eventually some awakening sense of honor on the part of her betrayer might cause him to right the wrong he had done her. But the King of Amarugia's sense of honor, if he had any, which is very doubtful, did not awaken, and he begn[sp] to plot more excuses to put the girl off. (Military Wedding, 1)

At this point Maud realized that drastic measures had to be taken and she called on the help of the Cass County Prosecuting Attorney, who, after hearing the story from Maud issued a warrant for Frank Hankins on a charge of rape. The warrant was given to Constable Tom Blackmon, who immediately left for Amarugia to arrest Hankins. The Constable. . .

. . . collared the young man on his throne at his home. The "King" blustered and stormed, and said he wasn't going to go and all that; but he went just the same and put on a very brave front until after a consultation with a lawyer, he learned what the penalty was for his crime. He then became exceedingly anxious to marry the girl he had wronged and save himself several long year's hard service in the penitentiary. (Military Wedding, 1)

The story concludes on a high note, I guess, as the Constable took the reluctant groom south to find Maud and brought her back to Harrisonville where they roused a minister who performed the marriage ceremony at dawn that morning. The writer of the article casts doubt on the success of the union concluding the article with the statement, "it is very doubtful if he will support her."

The Amarugian response to the newspaper story above was swift and clear. "King Hankins" was not the king of Amarugia, and his dishonorable actions would not have been tolerated in Amarugia. The kingdom's response was published a short two weeks later in a letter to the editor of the *Cass County News* which was published in their June 15, 1900, edition.

We are requested by several prominent people of our community to give the following in resentment of the careless manner the Democrat has exercised in speaking of us. It is as follows: In the Democrat under the date of May 31, we notice an account of Military Wedding, the groom reporting that he is the King of Amarugia.

We Amarugians deny that the said person is King of Amarugia. We will admit that he is King of a dominion called "Dosock," which extends from Jerry Dorsett's eastward. Amarugia extending westward.

We are loyal subjects to our sovereign "King David," renouncing all others, and we also bear the (what seems to some people almost unpardonable) the name of being fighters, not cowards, as the "King of Dosock" has proven himself to be, neither do we deny the charge of fighting because it is honorable, not disgraceful. One sound from our kingdom horn is sufficient to arouse the whole nation, armed and ready for duty. So when you send your shot at us, not matter in what manner, we are ready to defend ourselves and good name to the very last. You are doubtless aware that every little, low-down, mean act committed in other kingdoms is charged to the Amarugians. Remember, we have the oldest and best record of any kingdom around here.

The letter then continues with a claim about a fertile valley in the Bible called Amarugia, which I have been unable to find any reference to in the Bible. It then goes into some seemingly unrelated stuff about how the Egyptians were good at embalming. The writer wraps it all up with the following paragraph:

In conclusion, we trust that our ministers to other kingdoms will faithfully discharge their duty and ever be faithful to the Kingdom of Amarugia, we hope that the diplomats of other kingdoms will look well to justice and honor, thereby giving us our just dues. (Cass County News, 1900)

One thing this response illustrates; is that not all the residents of Amarugia were embarrassed to be from the area. It also shows that at least some of the residents fully embraced the idea of the kingdom and thus the concept and practice of having a king. Conversely, I think it also shows the lack of seriousness that people in other parts of the county took in regard to the concept of Amarugia having a King.

The writer of the original article makes light of Hankins being the king and apparently doesn't know that the current ruler of Amarugia was King David, who had been on the throne since at least 1894. See the map below which shows some of the other "kingdoms" that are mentioned in various records found of the area between 1890-1910. It does seem that this kingdom concept is largely centered around the Everett Township as all these kingdoms are found in that part of Cass County.

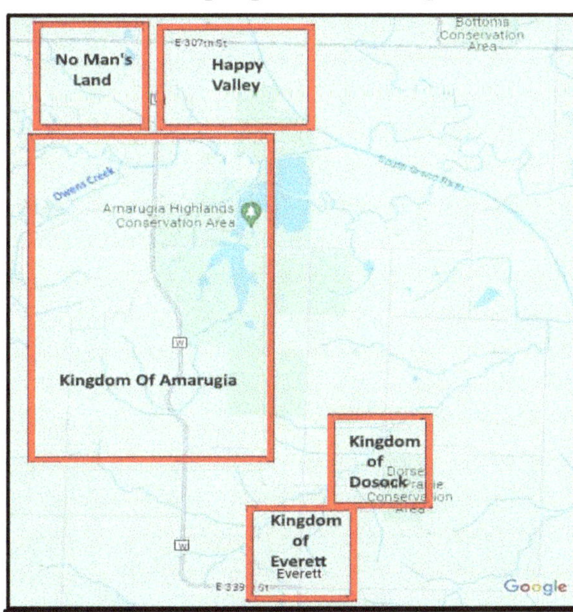

Figure 37:   Map of Kingdoms around Amarugia.   Likely around 1895–1900 timeframe.   Remember that King David expanded the Kingdom of Amarugia in 1894 to include the City of Everett. This change likely would have combined the Kingdom of Amarugia with the Kingdom of Everett.

Amarugia to the Outside World

Amarugia did not generally get a great deal of attention outside of Cass County, but when they did, it usually was not the positive press that they might have hoped for. One of the most famous residents of Amarugia was John Vivian Truman, the brother of United States President Harry S. Truman. John

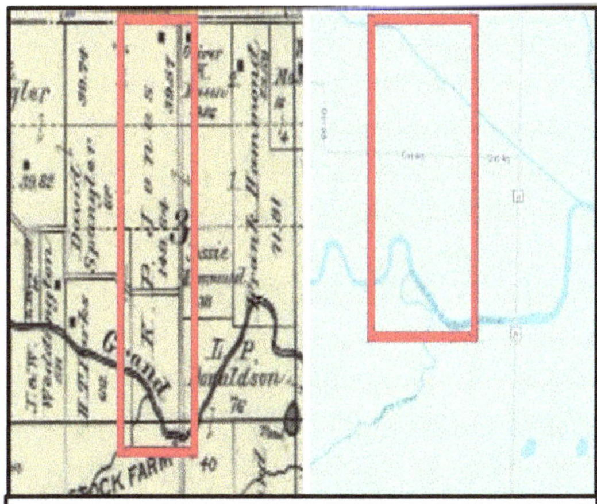

Figure 38: Left: 1912 Plat map shows the land owned by K.P. Jones. Which is where JV Truman lived and farmed in 1913-1914. Note that it appears that the plat map appears to say "Jonas" instead of Jones. I am attributing this to a spelling mistake. Right: Google map shows that same area today. It is likely the rivers have both changed a bit since 1912, but the area marked is very close to the same plot in 1912. (Courtesy Google Maps)

Figure 394: John Vivian Truman, 1886-1965,

Vivian is said to have relocated to Amarugia in 1913 to farm the land owned by Dr. K.P. Jones. Truman remembered Amarugia as a place "where the mud was so deep that a man could merely hold on the back of a horse drawn wagon and get it stuck". (Mystery Surrounds)

The 1949 article refers to Amarugia as an "unsavory place" and as late as 1950, Amarugia was characterized as of a "den of criminals and freeloaders". In an article published by the *Pawnee*

Chief Newspaper, Pawnee, Oklahoma, on January 5, 1950, the writer had some very unkind things to say about Amarugia, after it was discovered that Pawnee's previous Sheriff, George F. Feaster, was originally from Amarugia. The article jokingly wonders if Sheriff Feaster is a "furriner", which means foreigner. The writer then questions if it is legal for Feaster to hold office or vote in United States elections since he is a citizen of Amarugia and thus a foreigner.

The article contends that Sheriff Feaster,

. . . admits that he emigrated. The fact that he left there at night, pulling a good-sized black-jack bush after him to drag out his tracks, makes no difference now. The statute of limitations has run its course and there ain't nothing to fear no more. (Feaster, 2)

The Pawnee reporter then goes on to quote an uncited *Cass County Democrat-Missourian* article which tells the basic story of Amarugia being ruled by a king. The story continues to infer that the residents in Amarugia are a "sturdy lot" who can't be confined by sturdy walls. (i.e., they are criminals who should be in prison) The writer continues that the warden of the kingdom, who was tired of trying to chase the "escapees" down, gave up and decided that "living in Amarugia was punishment enough" for these poor souls. Poor souls who, by the way, are said to not wear socks or underwear in the wintertime. Nor do they eat cooked meat. (Feaster, 2)

I don't want to do injustice to the next paragraph of the article, which is interesting to say the least. For this reason, I have quoted it in its entirety.

Of recent years there has been an unconfirmed but persistent rumor that Amarugia has become sort of a purgatory for the lost and wandering spirits of deceased new dealers; kicked out of hades, they have sought a refuge there. On arrival a spirit receives a deep freeze and is promised a 5 per cent dividend on government contracts. Each contends the government owes it a living and refuses to make any effort to earn its own. The Amarugia government has run out of spending money, has taxed the rich out of existence and can't even borrow the money from itself. Famine results and when a famished spirit expires

it has purged and atoned itself in enduring the tortures of the land of Amarugia and is fit for something better. (Feaster, 1950)

When the Pawnee writer says, "new dealers", he is referring to supporters of President Franklin Delano Roosevelt's New Deal Program, which was one of the first social support programs enacted in the United States. Obviously, the writer of the article is not a fan of the New Deal and feels that beneficiaries of the program want to be cared for by the government and do not want to work to provide for themselves. Rather they expect the government to take care of all their needs. It seems clear that this article is a bit "tongue in cheek" but it is strange that they chose Amarugia to be a target for the New Deal analogy.

Folklore and Mystery

In more recent years, the area once known as the Kingdom of Amarugia has developed a reputation as an area with a relationship with the occult and other strange phenomena. While there are stories about such events there is very little hard evidence of any such events taking place. This reputation led to the area becoming a hotbed for young thrill seekers in the 1970s to treat the area as an ideal spot to congregate and indulge in legal and illegal substances. The altered state of mind also probably created more "strange" occurrences which were then brought back to the local schools making the area only more popular as a place to gather. With no real evidence, one might assume that the power of suggestion was really what fostered the reputation as that of a place where strange and mysterious things happened.

To be fair, the reputation and folklore of the area dates all the way back to the settling of the land when it was passed down from generation to generation that Ponce de Leon was present in the winter of 1513. Folklore says that de Leon spent a winter in Amarugia after traveling to Missouri from Florida. While in the area, he reportedly buried vast treasure. A treasure which people have been searching for over hundreds of years. (Western MO, 1987) A great story, but unfortunately, history tells us that Ponce de Leon was in the Bahamas in the winter of 1513, and it is very unlikely that he was in what would become western Missouri at the time. It is certainly possible that he was here at some other time, but there is no historical documentation that confirms or even alludes to that possibility.

Buried treasure is a common theme in the folklore that came out of Amarugia. Treasures hidden in the Amarugia hills have been attributed to various sources. The treasures were reportedly buried in Amarugia by Ponce de Leon, Civil War Bushwhacker, William Quantrill, Jesse James or Jesse's friend and local celebrity, Cole Younger. Again, folklore being what it is, there is no evidence that any of these men ever buried treasure in the area, but the stories passed from generation to generation have kept the tales of treasure alive in the Amarugia hills.

The Daily Journal quotes a resident in 1987 who says that "No one's ever found the treasure, naturally, because they don't know which hill to look in." (*The Daily Journal*, 1987)

Stories of Amarugia residents with special powers also added to the reputation the kingdom had across the rest of western Missouri. One man, Albert Osborn, (in Gross's book this man is identified as Grandad Horton) reportedly could magically stop bleeding. Allegedly, Albert helped a young girl who had cut herself quite severely and was bleeding profusely. The story goes that Albert took the girl's arm in his hands and said a few words. At that point, the bleeding mysteriously stopped.

Local lore says that Albert was often consulted by local residents in much the same way a doctor would be consulted. (Osborn, 8) Gross takes this story a step further and says that this man believed that his skill could only be passed on to a female. He reportedly tried to pass the techniques to his granddaughter, but she was unable to master the skills prior to her grandfather's death. (Gross, 26)

Another local celebrity, who Gross identifies as "Old Dot", was an elderly lady who could communicate with the dead by tapping on the floor. The spirits would then respond by making similar noises which the lady would then interpret for the person requesting to speak with their lost loved one. (Osborn, 7)

Almost all accounts and stories about Amarugia and the lore that surrounds the land include stories of the Ku Klux Klan and their activities in the area. My research has uncovered little to no evidence that the Ku Klux Klan was in Cass County prior to 1923. I have no doubt that there was likely Klan activity prior to that but I can find no written records to confirm that. One might say that it would be expected that I would not find any records since the Klan was a secretive organization and not a group who would publicize their activity. That may have been true in the early days after the Civil War, but the Klan's strategy apparently changed in 1923. Beginning in that year, I have found several articles about Klan activities. In 1923, the Klan became very public in sponsoring events, publicizing meetings, and announcing Klan rallies in local newspapers.

This work is not meant to be a history of the Klan in Cass County, but I wanted to share just a few articles that were published in 1923 to show the reader what was happening with the Klan in the area during this time. In June of 1923, The *Drexel Star* published an announcement under the heading, "Ku Klux Klan Notes", an article announcing the formation of a chapter of the Klan in the Drexel area. Highlights from the article are below:

Whereas, I have come into your city and have organized a provisional organization of the Knights of the Ku Klux Klan from among the most influential and highest type of men of your community. On their behalf and for your enlightenment by power invested in me by our Emperor, I issue the following statements:

The Knights of the Ku Klux Klan is essentially a secret and an invisible organization composed of American native born, white, gentile, protestant men over eighteen years of age and engaged in legitimate occupation, whose character and reputation are known by their fellow citizens to be good.

The writer then goes on to list some of the things that the Klan believes and teaches including, the Christian Religion, White Supremacy, the upholding of the Constitution of the United States, the sovereignty of our State Rights, the separation of Church and State, freedom of Speech and Press and preventing the causes of mob violence and lynchings. Another interesting point made by the writer is that he says that it is understood and expected by any active member of the Klan that if they are asked if they are a member, they will deny that membership. The article is signed by Oliver Royse, Sub. Khagh of Cass and Bates counties, Realm of Missouri of the Invisible Empire, the Knights of the Ku Klux Klan. (KKK Notes, 1923)

In Pleasant Hill, the paper announces a Klan lecture to be given at the Jesse Johnson farm on Happy Hill where the fiery cross of the Klan recently blazed. This attempt to change the public image of the Klan was taken a step further in February of 1924 when the Klan erected and paid for a large American flag and a 60-foot flagpole for the Peculiar public school. The *Cass County Democrat-Missourian* reported the gift concluding the article with:

Both the pole and flag were purchased and donated to the school by the Knights of the Ku Klux Klan of this place, and we feel sure that the school and community are more than appreciative of them. (Flagpole, 1924)

The article writer Lilly McClellen, says that the "KKK has used the Amarugia Highlands for their meetings." She continues by saying that this is not surprising since the KKK was a very prominent organization in Cass County. (McClellen, 2021) McClellen's thoughts on the Klan presence in the area are common, particularly in writings from the last 30 years or so. The term "prominent" is debatable, as there is little evidence of significant Klan activity in Amarugia. However, we do know that according to the aforementioned articles, the Klan did hold meetings in Drexel, which sits just outside Amarugia.

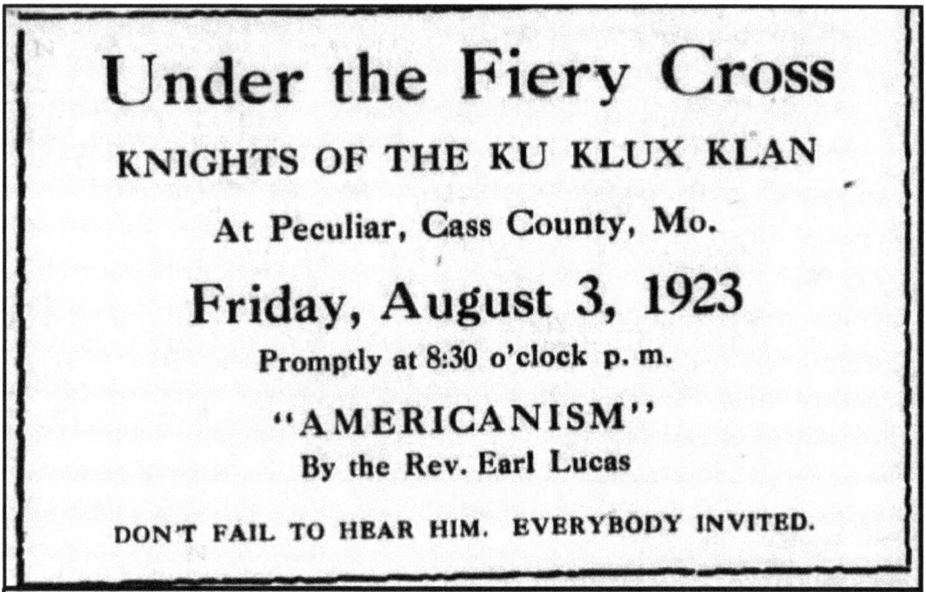

Under the Fiery Cross

KNIGHTS OF THE KU KLUX KLAN

At Peculiar, Cass County, Mo.

Friday, August 3, 1923

Promptly at 8:30 o'clock p. m.

"AMERICANISM"

By the Rev. Earl Lucas

DON'T FAIL TO HEAR HIM. EVERYBODY INVITED.

Figure 40: Announcement of KKK speech to be held in Peculiar in 1923. (The Cass County Democrat-Missourian, 1923)

We also know that the Klan held meetings across Cass County in the 1923–1925-time frame and that some of those meetings were reportedly quite well attended. The question of the significance of the Klan in the area is yet another one where we will likely never know the true answer. Could the Klan have been prominent? Yes. Were they? We just don't know for sure.

The Final Years of the Kingdom

I have found nothing in my research that tells me how long the second reign of King Jacob Weddington lasted. As was previously mentioned, he was already one of the older residents of the area when he accepted the crown for the second time around 1910. He only lived a few more years, passing away in 1916 at the age of 79.   During the period after King Jacob's reign, roughly between 1913 and 1920, the title seems to have been passed around quite frequently. This "passing of the crown" makes one wonder if the title, "King of Amarugia", while still used, took on connotations similar to that of "mayor" in many small towns. Another possibility is that by this time, the title had become a tongue in cheek reference to an important man in town.

The list below is a list compiled from published sources of men who at some point in the early 1900s were called the "King of Amarugia" by local media.

Evan Henten Fortner (1862-1922)

1913: *The Harrisonville Review and Cass County Leader* in December of 1913 informs that "J.T. Hensley's cousin, Mr. Fortner, **the king of Amarugia**, is visiting here this week."   Fortner was a long-time resident of Everett Township, appearing on census records from 1890-1920. He was also the son-in-law of King Jacob Weddington as he married Jacob's daughter Josephine "Josie" Weddington.

Charles H. Parish (1864-1928)

1917: *The Cass County Democrat-Missourian* in January of 1917 prints that "Charlie has been dubbed by some of his friends as the present **"King of Amarugia"**. Charles was the eldest son of H. H. Parish, who if you remember was one of the factions of political strife in the kingdom that led to the banishment of King Thomas Bundy in 1880. Charles sold "Meadowbrook Farms", one of the largest in Amarugia in 1917, and eventually moved to another farm four miles northwest of Harrisonville.

Lloyd L. Luckeman

All from the *Cass County Democrat-Missourian*

<u>March 1920</u>: "Lloyd L. Luckeman and family moved to their new home in "Amarugia" on Monday. We are sorry to lose these good people from this community but trust his office as "**King of Amarugia**" will not make him forget old friends and neighbors, and that we will see them back our way every once in a while."

<u>January 1921</u>: "Lloyd L. Luckeman, "**King of Amarugia**" was in Archie last Saturday for the express purpose of getting his DEMOCRAT, and also his neighbors' copies."

<u>September 1923</u>: "Lloyd Luckeman, **King of Amarugia**, and his wife returned recently from an auto trip to their old home in Illinois, and he is now a renewal subscriber to the DEMOCRAT.

Jerry Dorsett

I don't believe that Jerry Dorsett was ever the king but included him in this section due to an article in *The Cass County Democrat-Missourian* in July of 1901 that says that "Jerry Dorsett, the statesman from Everett and erstwhile **King of Amarugia**, was in Harrisonville the first of the week with a sample of oil taken from a well on the farm of E.W. Longwell." (Oil, 1901) I can find no other mention of him being the king except this single article.

The article refers to Dorsett as the "erstwhile king of Amarugia". I had to look up "erstwhile" to find out that it means "in the past". The only previous mention of Dorsett is in King David's Proclamation of 1894, where David names him the "Chief Adviser and Speaker of our Sovereign Pleasure" (Proclamation, 1895). Dorsett also served in the Missouri State Legislature for a single term in 1897-1898. It is possible that calling him the King, was just a nod to his exalted position as a State Senator from Amarugia prior to 1901.

Figure 41: Jerry H Dorsett

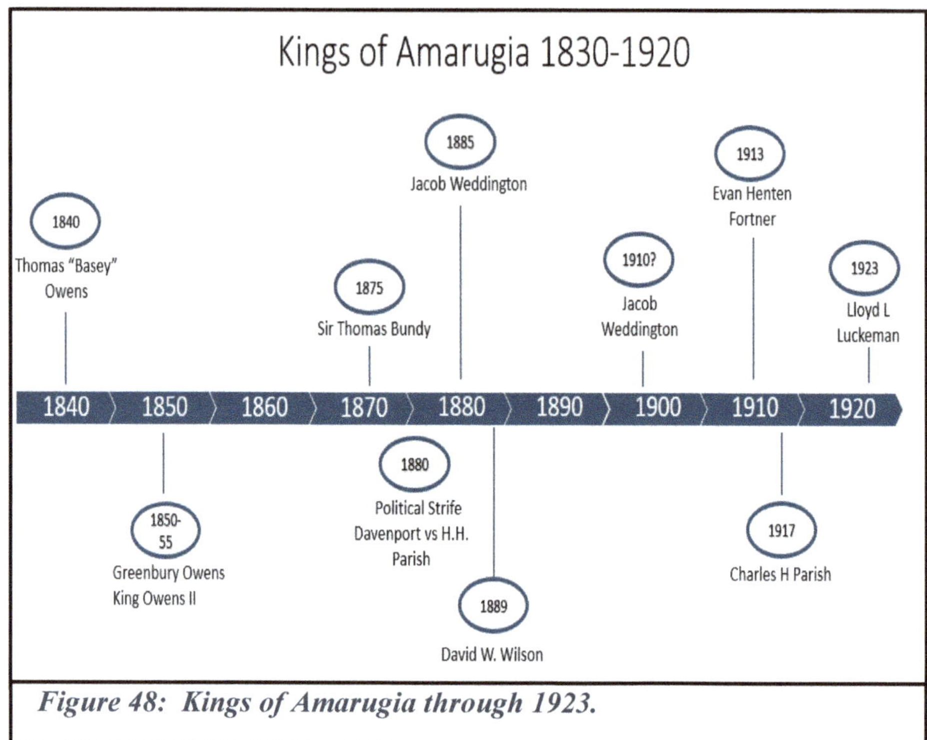

Figure 48: Kings of Amarugia through 1923.

Amarugia Today

The area that comprises the Kingdom of Amarugia is much different today than that which was ruled over by the kings of yesteryear. A large lake and conservation area now covers most of the eastern side of the highlands, the City of Everett has disappeared, all the old buildings are gone and of course any sign of a trading post has long been removed by the passage of time.

Being "from Amarugia" is largely a thing of the past and the name Amarugia has become a nostalgic reference for people who currently live in the area. Of course, anyone who was alive in the time of the kingdom has long been deceased. Today the once Kingdom of Amarugia now consists mainly of large rural farms and small homesteads set in the highlands and the prairie of southern Cass County.

In 1983, the Missouri Department of Conservation purchased 1081 acres in the heart of what had been the kingdom for the purpose of creating a large state conservation area. A 45-acre lake was built and

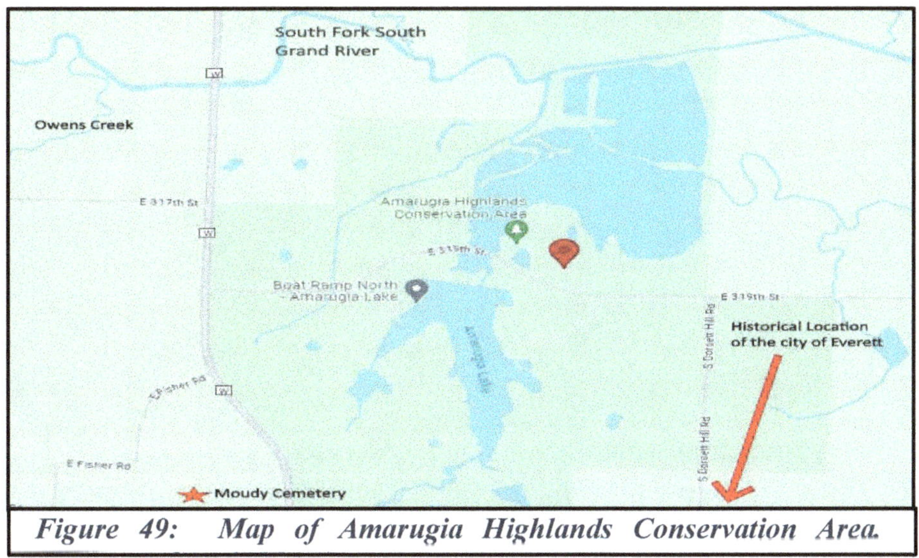

Figure 49:   Map of Amarugia Highlands Conservation Area.

stocked in 1987 when the conservation area was completed and opened to the public. According to Jim Gebhart, District Wildlife Supervisor at the time, "We'd like to try to maintain the history there that's worth preserving. Calling it Amarugia Highlands is one way to let the name live on." (Western Missouri, 1987) The Amarugia Highlands Conservation Area is open to the public and allows hiking, trap shooting, bird watching, hunting, fishing, and boating.

In 2014, the lake was dredged and renovated removing massive amounts of silt from the bottom. During that dredging, two automobiles were found under the water. One of them, a Cadillac, had possible bullet holes in the hood. No bodies were found, but the story only added to the lore of Amarugia. (KMBC.com)

Figure 43: Two submerged cars were discovered in the Amarugia Highlands lake when it was dredged in 2014. This image shows one of the cars with possible bullet holes in the hood.

Figure 42: Images of the Amarugia Highlands Conservation Area

Historically, there is no longer much to see if you are looking for items related to the kingdom. The one exception is the Moudy Cemetery, which was generally considered to be the preferred cemetery for those who lived in the "Highlands". The Everett Cemetery would have been the preferred location for those that lived in the "Prairie".

Moudy Cemetery, originally known as Herrell Cemetery, is thing from the days of the kingdom that still exists. This cemetery is not an easy one to find. It does not sit neatly along any road, and you will need to go through private property to get there. My daughter, Lexi, and I drove around for quite some time trying to locate the cemetery until as a last-ditch effort we stopped and talked to residents Danny Sanders and Steve Hamilton, who we happened to see talking in Danny's driveway. These two helpful gentlemen told us that the cemetery was about a half mile away and could only be accessed via a certain easement through the neighbor's land. They then offered to take us to the cemetery on their all-terrain vehicles. This form of transport is the only way we would have gotten to the site as the route involved fording a couple small creeks and steep hillsides. The cemetery is generally forgotten. We were told that locals, like Danny and Steve, sometimes go visit and run a weed eater around the graves. The earliest grave in this cemetery is that of Mary F. Jurd, who died April 22, 1857. The last burial in this

*Figure 44: Images of Moudy Cemetery. The image on the right shows Danny Sanders adjusting the sign at the entrance. No letters are visible on the sign. **This location is accessed through private property. Please check with homewoners before going through private property.*

cemetery was in the 1970s. Most of the graves date back to the late 1800s and early 1900s. Visitors to this site will see several names in this cemetery that have already been mentioned in this book. The most important might be the grave of two-time king, Jacob Weddington.

The Everett Cemetery, the preferred cemetery of the "Prairie People", is much easier to find. Located just east, on East 339 St (Route W), of the historical location of the town of Everett. The Everett Cemetery appears to have been created about 10 years after the Moudy

Figure 45: Everett Cemetery, East 339th St.

Cemetery. The earliest grave in this cemetery is that of Mary A Morton, who died October 4, 1868. This cemetery is still cared for and still active today. (Western Missouri, 87). While Everett Cemetery may have originally been preferred by the Prairie people, the creation of the city of Everett in 1867, and later the movement of the kingdom by King David in 1894 to that city, made the distinction between the highland residents and prairie folk less important. At that time any stigma about being buried in one cemetery versus another was likely diminished.

While the physical remnants of the Kingdom of Amarugia have faded with time, the mystery and folklore of the story still remains interesting to locals and outsiders alike. The City of Archie honored the memory of the area in the early 1980s, when they commissioned local artist Bev Roberts to memorialize the beauty of the Amarugian Highlands by painting a mural on the wall of the library in downtown Archie. The mural, which took about a month to complete, still exists today, although it is a bit weathered, and the building is no longer a library.

Figure 46: Mural of the Amarugia Highlands, painted by Bev Roberts. I have been unable to confirm the exact date of the creation of the mural, but I believe it to be in the early 1980s.

Analysis of the Kingdom

The story of the Kingdom of Amarugia is a strange, fascinating, and fun story. After getting past the crazy idea of a king ruling a kingdom in the middle of Missouri, what can we make of the true story of Amarugia? Was it a functioning government that held and wielded power, dealt with enemies, and doled out their own brand of justice? Or was it simply a small group of people who lived by the rules and guidelines of a government not officially recognized by any level of established government that existed in the area? Or was it just a kooky club that local residents belonged to? A club, which like other social clubs, had certain rules and regulations that members were expected to abide by.

To wrap up this examination of the Kingdom of Amarugia, I'm going to lay out the case for each of these possibilities. I would remind you that I don't have the absolute answer to these questions. My goal with this chapter, and the book overall, is to provide the information for each possibility and then allow the reader to make their own decision based on the facts already presented.

Was the Kingdom a functioning government existing among other local governments? Was it a government entity that possessed the power to make treaties with other "kingdoms", enforce rules, pass judgement, and administer punishment on those that did not abide by those rules? When considering this possibility, we must consider who held that power for the rest of the state. The reality is that when King Owens I established the Amarugian monarchy with himself as king in or around 1840, there was already a functioning county, state, and federal government at the time. Could the Kingdom of Amarugia really exist alongside these other levels of government? To be fair, Cass County and most of western Missouri at the time was very sparsely populated, and it is likely that the existing forms of government, and more importantly, local law enforcement, were probably not seen on a regular basis in or near the remote areas of Amarugia.

This lack of a consistent law enforcement presence makes possible the idea that the residents of Amarugia needed some alternative form of local legal authority. Human nature tells us that settlers in this remote region would have had disagreements. There would also be some among the settlers who felt like the laws of organized society did not apply to them and if they could steal or cheat to get what they wanted they would do so. For this reason, it is not far-fetched to think that some form of local government and law enforcement would have been needed by law-abiding citizens to help keep things civil.

Earlier in the book, it is discussed how many transgressions occurred between the "prairie people" and the "highlanders". These crimes, mostly minor in nature, such as the stealing of chickens or firewood, would likely not be something that would justify a trip by the County Sheriff to the area. In the 1800s a trip for the Sheriff from Harrisonville to Amarugia, would have been a two-day round trip on horseback. For this reason, I think it is fair to assume that the Cass County Sheriff was not coming out for each and every complaint from either side of these small disputes.

The fact that the early settlers chose a monarchy as their form of government is not a great surprise as many of the early settlers, pre-1850, or their parents had likely emigrated from European countries where monarchies were common. The familiarity with this form of government meant that it was understood. A monarchy was also a government that would not be difficult to implement. On the cynical side, this government structure also gave the selected leaders the ability to bestow upon themselves fancy titles and powers that most of these low born settlers would enjoy having.

Also realize that a monarchy with one person in charge was a very easy form of government to implement and keep in place. Contrast that to a democracy where elections would have to be organized and held. Rules to govern those elections and the people elected would have to be put into place. There would also need to be a way to enforce those rules. The reality of the times was that these early settlers spent their days trying to survive. It was a difficult life where hard work was expected of them every day. They didn't have time to create and run a democratic government. For this reason, having one person to take on the "administration" of the area would likely have been an attractive way to organize their society.

As time goes on, the idea of a monarchy gets a little harder to understand. If we consider the time of the Civil War, we know that

Amarugia, while still remote, would have had a great deal more traffic with Union Troops, Bushwhackers and Jayhawkers making regular trips throughout the area. This traffic, particularly by Union troops, makes the need for a single person to dole out justice a bit less likely. As the time passed from King Owen I in 1850 through King Thomas Bundy, who ruled until around 1880, it is possible and likely that the powers and authority granted to the kings were gradually reduced as the presence and effectiveness of local law enforcement agencies became more consistent.

In Robert Gross' fictional book, he implies that the king had the power to execute people who broke the rules of the kingdom. I find the idea that even in King Owens I's reign from 1840-1850, that the recognized local law enforcement would simply ignore a person in their county ordering someone to be executed without an actual trial by a government recognized court to be highly unlikely. On the other hand, the idea that the first few kings would have been allowed to pass sentences on certain minor offenses with a punishment such as bastinado, caning of the feet, seems a bit more likely. It's possible that as long as the people in Amarugia were happy with how minor offenses were being handled, the local sheriff would simply not get involved except in the more serious offenses.

If we assume this reduction in the power of the Kings over time to be true, it tracks that the later kings may have had very little true enforcement power. It seems probable that by this time, the king was more like the leader of a local homeowner's association or HOA. The kings in the latter years of the kingdom probably were making decisions, not so much about crimes and outside enemies, but instead about minor transgressions like when a resident failed to live up to the expectations of being a good neighbor.

Even if this evolution of the role is true, it is still quite remarkable that the residents appear to have "bought in" to the idea of a kingdom and to the power of the king. Imagine if someone came to you today and said we are going to start a club that is going to make rules about how you manage your property and you are going to be required to follow the rules we come up with. That would probably not go over too well.

But in Amarugia, this appears to have been the case as records tell us that these "royal subjects" abided by the rulings of the kings over the 70 or 80 years that the kingdom existed. We can see an example of this acceptance by reviewing the thoughts of the author of the letter to the editor in 1900, written in response to the "Military Wedding" story in the *Cass County Democrat-Missourian*. The writer makes it clear that he or she is very proud to be an Amarugian and to be a subject of King David. This "buy in" by the residents which seems to have been consistent until at least 1900 is astonishing given that there was no legal reason why the residents would have had to abide by the rules of the kingdom. But they did.

We can also see in this letter that by 1900, despite the negative opinions of Amarugia seen in local papers, Amarugians took pride in where they were from and were willing to stand up and defend themselves.

The last explanation of the story of the kingdom is that these people who created and continued to abide by the rules of the kingdom were just crazy, almost cult-like. In more modern days Amarugia did begin to have the reputation as a place where cult activity would take place. There is no hard evidence that there was ever any of this sort of activity in the area, but the concept may have been driven by an original idea that any group that would allow themselves to be ruled by a king resembled cult-like thinking. Once an area gets such a reputation, it is sometimes hard to shake the labels and ideas that come with that reputation.

Were the Amarugians just a bunch of crazy folks? Maybe. Again, the decision is up to each reader to make their own judgment of what to make of this story. My take is no, they were not crazy. At the beginning, they needed an easy way to control petty crimes and misdeeds by the residents without the physical presence of full-time law enforcement. They found the ability to control those elements of their society in the absolute monarchy system that they implemented.

After they established this form of local government and it worked, it may have simply become a way of life for the residents. If you moved into the area, there was probably significant peer pressure in a "this is the way we do it" kind of thinking. As a newcomer, if you wanted to be accepted by your neighbors, you fell in line. I'm sure that over time there were people who did not fall in line, but we don't see any records of those people. Remember that both King David and King Bundy were eventually run out of the area for their transgressions. If the king could be banished, there is no reason to believe that a normal person couldn't be expelled also. That said, there are no official records of this occurring, but the stories of the two kings makes this practice a very real possibility.

The stories of also tell us that certain kings took their role and title more seriously than others. King David seems to have taken pride in his role as king and greatly enjoyed the title and fame that came with it. On the other hand, Jacob Weddington, seems to have been a much more low-key ruler and may have taken the crown, two times, simply because no one else was going to do it. Near the end of the kingdom, after 1910, the title of king seems to have become less of an official title and more of a moniker that was used to describe someone who was a leader in the area.

I decided to write this book after I wrote a post on my website, www.jonathanjonesauthor.com, which told the basic story. That post is still the most popular post that I have ever done. I think that a significant part of the interest comes from the mysterious nature of the area and the idea that people in a very rural part of Missouri could form and maintain their own government. After researching the history and identifying the real people and the reasons for the kingdom, I fear that I may be ruining the intrigue. Intrigue that I think is heightened, by the unknown nature of the strange story.

To those who enjoy history and facts, I hope you enjoyed the book and leave with a clearer historical explanation of what may have happened in Amarugia. To those who want to keep the mystery of the kingdom alive with visions of kings sitting on thrones, royal blood lines, and disputes between neighboring kingdoms, remember that many of the stories presented are simply inferences gathered from vague references to the kingdom over time. For those people, I encourage you to keep the fairy tale alive and ignore everything presented in this book. Long live the Kingdom of Amarugia!

The success of a self-published author is driven by online reviews of their work. If you enjoyed this book, a written review on any of the below sites would be greatly appreciated. If you didn't enjoy it, please ignore the links below 😊 .

www.goodreads.com

www.amazon.com

www.barnesandnoble.com

Bibliography

"Amaru." www.*mythlok.com*, Otiose Minds Media, mythlok.com/amar
u/. Accessed 29   Dec. 2023.

"Amarugia Boasts." *Cass County Democrat*-Missourian [Harrisonville
], 20 May 1886.

"Amarugia Echoes." *Cass County Democrat-Missourian* [Harrisonvill
e], 21 Sept 1916.

"Amarugia Echoes." *Cass County Democrat-Missourian* [Harrisonvill
e], 18 January 1917.

"Amarugia Echoes." *Cass County Democrat-Missourian* [Harrisonvill
e], 20 July 1911.

"Amarugia Echoes." *Cass County Democrat-Missourian* [Harrisonvill
e], 11 March 1920.

"Amarugia Echoes." *Cass County Democrat-Missourian* [Harrisonvill
e], 6 January 1921.

"Amarugia Echoes." *Cass County Democrat-Missourian* [Harrisonvill
e], 6 Sept 1923.

"Amarugia Echoes." *Cass County Democrat-Missourian* [Harrisonvill
e], 26 April 1928.

"Amarugia Echoes." *Harrisonville Review and Cass County Leader* [
Harrisonville], 11 Dec 1913

"Amarugia Hills Area to Be Permanent Prairie." *The Belton Star-Hera
ld* [Belton], 15 Dec 1977.

"Amarugia Items." *The Cass News* [Harrisonville], 15 June 1900.

"Amarugia legend comes into its own in Archie." *Kansas City Star* [K
ansas City], 14 May 2005, pp. 1+.

Barnard, Dora. "I Heard That." *The Missourian* [Harrisonville], 4 Mar
1980."Kingdom of Poosey." *The Missourian* [Harrisonville], 28 M
ar 1948.

Bradley, Donald. "'Amarugia' Never Existed But Always Was Real."
Cass County
Democrat [Harrisonville], 24 Nov 1949

Cass County Library. *Burial Sites and Cemeteries of Everett Township Cass County*. 1972.

"David W. Wilson Dead." *The Missourian* [Harrisonville], 3 Aug 1933.

Davis, Ted. *"The History of Everett"*. 1996.

"Death of Jacob Weddington." *Cass County Democrat-Missourian* [Harrisonville], 19 July 1916.

"Death of Jerry H. Dorsett." *Cass County Democrat-Missourian* [Harrisonville], 26 Oct 1917.

Drained Cass County Lake yields cars, mystery. *KMBC.com*, 5 Dec. 2012, www.kmbc.com/article/drained-cass-county-lake-yields-cars-mystery/3673367. Accessed 25 Mar. 2024.

"DW Wilson" *Cass County Democrat* [Harrisonville], 2 Jan 1919.

"A Drunk Named Owens." *Cass County Democrat* [Harrisonville], 24 May 1900.

"Flagpole." *The Cass County Democrat-Missourian* [Harrisonville, Missouri], 7 February 1923.

"George F. Feaster." *The Pawnee Chief* [Pawnee], 5 Jan 1950.

Glenn, Alan. *The History of Cass County*. Cass County, The National Historical Company, 1917.

Gross, Robert L. *Amarugia*. Madison, Southern Lion Book, 2009.

Gupta, Himanee. "Once upon a time, legends ruled in Cass County." *Kansas City Star* [Kansas City], 31 Jul 1987.

"Historical Group Studies 'Kingdom of Amarugia' *The Star Herald* [Belton, Missouri]. 27 Aug 1970.

History and Directory of Cass County, Missouri. Harrisonville, *Cass County Leader*, 1908.

"A History of Amarugia." *Cass County Democrat* [Harrisonville], 7 Feb 1899.

Johnson, Bernice I. "Place Names in Six of the West Central Counties of Missouri." M.A. thesis, University of Missouri-Columbia. 1933.

"Kingdom of Amarugia." *St. Louis Post-Dispatch* [St. Louis], 5 Oct 1994.

"Kingdom of Amarugia." *professorhex.blogspot.com*, 25 Nov. 2009, professorhex.blogspot.com/2009/11/ kingdom-of-amarugia.html. Accessed 23 Dec. 2023.

"Kingdom of Amarugia." *The Vandalia Leader* [Vandalia, Missouri], 14 Jan 1897.

"Kingdom of Poosey." *The Missourian* [Harrisonville], 28 Mar 1948.

"Ku Klux" Lecture Monday Night." *The Pleasant Times* [Pleasant Hill , Missouri], 18 May 1923.

"Ku Klux Klan Notes." *The Drexel Star* [Drexel Missouri], 21 June 1923.

"Ku Klux Klan Organized Here?." *The Drexel Star* [Drexel Missouri], 14 June 1923.

Lethcho, Tom. "Mystery surrounds region's origin" *St Joseph News-Press* [St Joseph, Missouri], 24 Oct 1997.

"Letter from Amarugia" *The Cass County News* [Harrisonville], 15 June 1900.

McClellan, Lilly. "The Amarugia Highlands of Cass County Missouri." Clio: Your Guide to History. December 15, 2021. Accessed May 8, 2023. https://theclio.com/entry/141792

McDonnel, James. Interview. Conducted by Jonathan Jones, 5 April. 2024.

"A Military Wedding, The 'King of Amarugia' Takes Himself a Bride." *Democrat* [Harrisonville], 31 May 1900.

"Missouri House of Representatives Adopted Dorsett Resolution." *Cass County Democrat-Missourian* [Harrisonville], 3 April 1919.

"Mrs. Hersie H. Parish." *Cass County Democrat* [Harrisonville], 28 Feb 1918.

"Mystery surrounds region's origin." *St. Joseph News-Press* [St. Joseph], 24 Oct 1997.

"Oak Hamilton Was Released." *Cass County Democrat* [Harrisonville] , 13 Dec 1917.

O'Bryan, Tony. "Jayhawkers." *Civil War on the Western Border*, Kansas City Public Library, civilwaronthewesternborder.org/encyclopedia/jayhawkers. Accessed 26 Mar. 2024.

"Oil at Everett" *Cass County Democrat-Missourian* [Harrisonville], 25 July 1901.

Osborn, Donald Lewis. *Tales of the Amarugia Highlands*. Lee's Summit, 1972.

Plat book of Cass County, Missouri. Philadelphia, A.R. Stinson, 1912. State Historical Society of Missouri, https://digital.shsmo.org/digital/collection/plat/id/7982/rec/2. Map.

"Prosperity in Cass County." *Cass County Democrat* [Harrisonville], 23 July 1903.

Reeves, Ruth Schuller. "Just over the Hill." *Missouri Conservationist*, July 1990, pp. 14-17.

"Royal Proclamation" *Cass County Democrat-Missourian* [Harrisonvi
lle], 8 March 1894

Scott, Donna. "It's a Brush Arbor Meeting." *Bittersweet*, vol. 3, no. 1, f
all 1975.

Shipley, Stephen. Interview. Conducted by Jonathan Jones, 31 Mar. 20
24.

"Tales of Amarugia." *The Daily Journal* [Flat River], 15 Sept 1987.

The History of Cass County. Cass County, The National Historical Co
mpany, 1883.

"The Stern Visitations of War in Cass County." *CassCoLibrary.org*, C
ass County Public Library,
www.casscolibrary.org/casscountyhistory/panel1/. Accessed 25 Ma
r. 2024.

"Walter Rogers" *Cass County Democrat* [Harrisonville], 6 April 1911.

"We Have Been Having 'Louse Rains." *Cass County Democrat*[Harris
onville, Missouri], 22 June 1916, p. 7.

Wells, Harold F, compiler. *Civil War Veterans of Cass County Missou
ri*. Harrisonville.

"We Have Been Having "Louse Rains" *Cass County Democrat-Misso
urian* [Harrisonville], 22   June 1916.

"Western Missouri Highlands rich in folk tales of Amarugia." *Columbi
a Daily Tribune* [Colum- bia, Missouri], 6 Dec 1987, pg. 46.

"Wilson Homecoming." *Cass County Democrat* [Harrisonville], 10 Jul
y 1919.

Wise, Marie. "The Challenge of Genealogy." *The Daily Advertiser* [La
fayette], 6 Feb 1980.

Woolridge, John. "Amarugia Kings." *Cass County Times* [Harrisonvill
e, MO], 19th ed., 1 Jan.   1887.

About the Author

Jonathan Jones was born and raised in Harrisonville, Missouri. He graduated from Missouri State University with a BS in Business Education and later earned an MBA in International Business from Park University. Jones spent ten years as a teacher and coach in Missouri Schools before moving into the business world where he has spent the last 20+ years working as a business architect for IAT Insurance Group. Jones is a lifelong history buff and spends much of his spare time researching history, both in his local area as well as traveling to visit historic sites around the world. Jones and his wife of 34 years, Jill, have three grown children, Zac, Lexi, and Nikai and currently live in Olathe, Kansas. More information about Jones' work can be found by visiting www.JonathanJonesAuthor.com.